2

4

THE CHOSEN

LESSONS LEARNED FROM ADOPTION

THE
CHOSEN

LESSONS LEARNED FROM ADOPTION

BY

MICHELLE NEELY WILSON

8

Psalm 27

Of David.

[1] The LORD is my light and my salvation—
whom shall I fear?
The LORD is the stronghold of my life—
of whom shall I be afraid?

[2] When the wicked advance against me
to devour[a] me,
it is my enemies and my foes
who will stumble and fall.
[3] Though an army besiege me,
my heart will not fear;
though war break out against me,
even then I will be confident.

[4] One thing I ask from the LORD,
this only do I seek:
that I may dwell in the house of the LORD
all the days of my life,
to gaze on the beauty of the LORD
and to seek him in his temple.
[5] For in the day of trouble
he will keep me safe in his dwelling;
he will hide me in the shelter of his sacred tent
and set me high upon a rock.

THE LIBRARY OF CONGRESS

The Chosen

Lessons Learned from Adoption

ISBN:

978-1-7361725-0-6

Printed in the United States

FOREWARD - Sibling Love

Siblings don't always come to us through blood, they sometimes come to us through love, close relationships, and by way of blended family bonds. The latter is how I gained my adopted little sister. No, we didn't live in the same home, no we didn't share the same parents, but what we do share is a sibling bond. It was a beautiful day when I first learned from my then best friend that we, yes, I said we (what was his was mine and what was mine was his) had a new little sister. I use the term we because everyone in the community was family. But how could we have a little sister? His mother was not expecting a child. I knew this because in my eight-year-old mind I was smart enough to know what a pregnant lady looked like and my best friend's mother was not pregnant. The very next day I was introduced to the term "adoption" and to a brand-new baby girl named Michelle.

No one could have imagined the joy I had when I learned about adoption. A brand-new baby for me to play with, love, and adore. That was when I decided to adopt my baby sister. As any good sibling/big sister would do I carefully watched her grow into the beautiful woman she is today. As the years passed, we have grown together, celebrated together, we've experienced loss together, and we have become siblings.

Living in a world where blended families are very much the norm, adoption is a wonderful option for completing a family. Michelle, who was adopted at birth has embraced all the blessings and love that her family had to offer to her. She lives her life daily by understanding that you are given only one chance at a happy life. Michelle is not defined by the circumstances of her birth. How she lives life has contributed to her success as a mother, wife, sibling, employee, sorority sister, and friend. She chose to not worry about the past but instead to enjoy every minute of the present. To know her is to see sunshine every day. Her passion for loving life is infectious and she spreads the joy of life everywhere she visits. You will find her view on adoption both inspiring and courageous. She is open and truthful about the void some feel as an adoptee but has chosen to share her journey about how she loves the life she was afforded by the family who chose to love her. You will walk away inspired as you learn about her journey.

Love you more Michelle,
Big Sissy

Introduction

I was inspired to write this book based on my personal experience in the world of adoption. I wanted to be able to reach both children and adults with my story. Many people can create a family unit naturally. There is also the population that no matter how hard they try; it just never comes to pass. Some families are equipped to naturally give birth, yet still expand their families using other methods. In today's world, there are so many options available to help families grow and we are grateful for them all. It is no longer a one-stop shop for everyone. You now can choose the path which fits your lifestyle. It just so happens that my journey included being adopted as a newborn. Over the next several chapters of this book, I intend to share my deepest innermost feelings and all the emotions that I have experienced along the way.

Adoption is the process through which a person — the adoptive parent — assumes permanent legal responsibility for a child. Adoption requires the biological parents (the ones responsible for the birth of the child) to give up their legal right to custody of their child. Today, three types of adoptions may be chosen: "closed," "semi-open" and "open." These terms describe the approximate level of contact and interaction that the birth mother can expect to have with the adoptive parents and the child during the adoption process and afterward. My adoption was closed.

Most are not aware of their entry point of coming into a family. Some are probably wondering why don't I look like my mom, dad, or the rest of the family. Now there could be a million reasons why that is, and adoption may not necessarily be on that list. Then there is the group who were adopted, always knew they were adopted, and still ponder the million-dollar question: WHY? The answers to these questions could vary, but whatever the reason, I say to those of you who were adopted hold your head up high. Stick your chest out and be proud because regardless of the reason, you were **CHOSEN**.

Adoption impacts everyone differently. No matter the role in the process, whether you are the adoptee, the parents adopting or the parents giving up a child for adoption, there is a power you bring to the equation, and it should be embraced as a blessing. I desire to help those that have walked this path to see and understand how much of a blessing your role truly is and to have it bring you happiness and inspiration because of this life-changing experience. Do we tend to always lean toward the unanswered questions that focus solely on the Why? And the what-ifs? When what we should be focusing on is being present in our space of being blessed beyond measure. I am hopeful my journey of being adopted as a newborn will help another adoptee embrace and love the fact; that they too were adopted. There is power in being chosen. For me, it feels like there is a higher calling to help others who may struggle with this reality. And this calling has multiple phases and desired outcomes. Primarily to enlighten others about adoption and bring awareness and community to those who may feel they are on this journey alone. For the parents that gave up a child for adoption, my hope is for you to feel guilt-free about the decision you made based on the circumstances you faced at that time. Equally important, are those families that opened their hearts and homes offered themselves as a blessing to a child, and took on the journey to increase your family by adopting. Thank you! I am personally so grateful to you for your unconditional love. No matter your part in the equation, you are all the real Most Valuable Players in the world of adoption.

Today, I have a beautiful family, married to my wonderful husband Reginald Wilson of five years. We are truly the definition of what a match made in heaven describes. Two very imperfect people who together are nothing less than perfection. We push and pull each other just at the right times. And somehow even when we do not agree we always meet in the middle. It is now more than five years later that we joined in holy matrimony, and I am still amazed and grateful that GOD blessed us to find each other. This union blessed me with three wonderful bonus children and five beautiful grandchildren. Our youngest daughter Neely Simone was my contribution to our blended family. She has made her transition to college life which will officially render us, empty nesters. Oh, and let me not forget our spoiled fur babies Neiman Elizabeth "The Queen" and Marcus Alexander "The Great" two beautiful Goldendoodles who rule the house. Most think that I married late in life, and I agree, but that is what worked best for me.

Although an adjustment for my daughter, we have settled in quite well as a family.

Nearly twelve full years of being a duo and then suddenly you are a trio is a lot for anyone I would imagine. For the first three years like clockwork, we ate breakfast and dinner together as a family. This was intentional for me because it allowed us to have that quality time together as a family and my mind could rest knowing they both had two good meals a day. That fourth year I begin to cut the cord a bit with the youngest to let her test her wings on preparing herself for the day. Such as making her breakfast and organizing her school needs for the day. My professional career has been spent in Human Resources leadership where I am currently supporting multiple States as the Human Resources Manager for a global company that focuses on Engineering, Architecture, and Environmental Construction services.

A native Houstonian and graduate of Prairie View A&M University a large part of my life has been spent serving the community through many service organizations. In my spare time, I love spending time with my family, entertaining, cooking, traveling, and enjoying life to the fullest. Although this is a true snapshot of my current life today; the road was not always easy. There were so many twists and turns, ups and downs, and many over-the-top wins and it all started with me being CHOSEN. This shaped me and has been a force that has brought me to where I am today.

As previously mentioned, I wanted to reach both children and adults who have been adopted. Along with parents on both sides of the equation. Specifically, those that decided to adopt and those who decided to give their child up for adoption. I desire to offer some insight on the process of adoption and recommendations on how to potentially handle it no matter your role. If by chance this book finds its way into the hands of someone who has zero insight into the process and has no experience on either side; being adopted or adopting. Perhaps it will help in the event you encounter someone who has been adopted or has adopted a child to handle that relationship with a more informed level of care. For those adoptees seeking to find their birth families; it is my goal to help you understand that what you may be envisioning your experience to be when you meet your birth family could be light-years in contrast to what you discover if ever afforded the opportunity. Many adoptees never seek to find their biological parents. I would imagine it's mostly due to the fear of rejection and possibly a fear of what you will find at the end of the path. We have all seen the feel-good storylines on television of long-lost parents, children, and siblings finding each other after years and years of searching along with the anticipation, tears, and excitement that are all heartwarming. Although, I do not claim to know the actual statistics on how these meetings turn out long-term; I am hopeful that the positive outweighs the negative.

Whatever your reason for your journey please make sure you are happy within because like everything else it all starts there. Your happiness is not predicated on meeting your birth parents, no more than happiness can magically appear when one gets married or divorced. Each of these examples is different, but the message is the same. Our love of self must be solid. You must indeed love yourself before you can love another person. The pressure for someone else to make you happy is too great a responsibility. Not speaking from a physical appearance but from that of your soul. As women, we love make-up, weaves, wigs, and trying new things with our hair, fingernails, and make-up applications. Change happens so regularly in my house my husband must often wonder, who will I wake up to day-to-day? But when stripped of all those things and you stand in the all-natural self. Do you love what GOD created? As a young girl, I cannot say for sure that I understood my journey. However, now fifty-plus years old having made my way through my path of life to this point it is truly clear that I certainly love myself. I am grateful for the journey GOD designed just for me.

When I say you must love yourself and be happy with yourself that is exactly what I mean. When there is no one else in the room, no audience, no family just you alone stripped of the fancy house, the expensive cars, the designer clothes and handbags, the degrees on the wall, everything. How do you feel about who you are as a person? This is paramount for anyone adopted or not. But more so important for anyone looking to find a life partner, have a family, or introduce a new friend into your life that has not always been a part of your daily fabric.

CHAPTER ONE

THE FIRST REVEAL – YOU ARE ADOPTED!

I was adopted as a baby girl by two loving parents Michael and Betty Neely. In the late 1960's I was only three months old in this world when my life was changed forever. There are many things that you remember as a child. Special occasions, birthday parties, playdates, life accomplishments, and those traumatic experiences such as the death of loved ones. I remember it as though it happened as recently as yesterday. My mother called me into the family room. Back then we called it the "den." She was very crafty and loved making things. One of her gifts was interior design. We lived in a middle-class neighborhood in a relatively spacious home for a family of four. Everyone had their room, and my room was particularly special to me because it doubled as my play space and was very frilly and girly. Imagination was key for me being the baby and ten years younger than my older brother. I played by myself often and my Barbie mansions were the business and toys were unlimited. My mother sewed as a hobby and continuously changed the décor of our home from as far back as I can remember. Hence, so did the décor of my Barbie mansions. On this day she was cutting out a pattern for curtains she was making for the formal living room when she called me to come to talk. Doing my usual playing with my dolls in my room. Her summoning me was nothing new or out of the ordinary as we always had the best girl talks about anything and everything. It rained this day, and I was not able to go outside and play which was one of the reasons I happened to be in the house. It seemed convenient and the perfect time to have the talk I am sure were her thoughts.

As I entered the room she said, come sit with mommy. I want to explain something to you and if you have any questions please do not hesitate to ask. She went on to explain that although I was her daughter, and she was my mother she wanted me to know that another wonderful woman carried me in her belly for nine months. She decided to give you up at birth because at the time she could not adequately care for and provide for you. And through her bold and selfless act, your dad and I were blessed and given the honor of being your parents through a process called adoption. We adopted you at three months old and instantly fell in love. And have loved you ever since the day we met you. From that day on you have been ours and that will never change. She went on to tell me that if I ever wanted to know who my biological parents were, she and my dad would do everything in their power to support and assist me with finding them. But be clear and have no doubt you were born from our hearts and not my belly, but you are ours. Hearing this as a child was very scary and eyes wide open shocking and unraveling just to describe a few of the many things I felt like learning this information for the first time. At that moment everything I knew to be facts was now different, yet it was still the same. Then I instantly jumped to the thought "is she going to come back and try to take me?" I knew at that moment that I did not want to leave, but what if she came back and tried to steal me? Does she know where I live? As my mother continued to explain this new phenomenon, adoption to me. She was able to do so with precision equal to that of a brain surgeon performing that initial incision on the scalp. She had details of the location, date, and time of my delivery that she shared. It was all documented for my eyes to see, and I could read it on what were the legal documents she shared. I could see that I was born at 1:34 PM in the early days of September. My mother also shared with me that she and my dad gave me my name Michelle Denise, which was different from the name my birth mother gave me. It was important to my parents that I be named after my dad.

I was very sickly as an infant and needed a lot of medical attention. The transparency continued, my mom went on to explain that before my arrival, she and my dad tried unsuccessfully to grow our family. After failing and suffering multiple miscarriages, they turned to the option of adoption. So now I am in the know about my adoption. My young four-year-old head was swirling trying to digest this information and understand what it all meant. After the initial shock and the ultimate scare reflecting on how carefully my mother delivered that message with such precision and know today how delicate and thoughtful, she was with her delivery. My sense of calm and belonging was restored very quickly. I am sure that it was her hope and expectation when she decided to share this earth-shattering life-changing news. Just an opinion, but my mom knew that she and my dad had provided for and loved me in a way that no matter what she shared with me the safety net had already been firmly planted. There was a solid foundation that even I could see as a child. The care, the dotting, the inclusion, and the feeling of belonging were all there. My mom checked back with me a week or so later and asked if I had any questions. Once it was established that I was safe and no one could just show up and take me, I was good. My adoption was closed, so my birth mother had no idea where

I was and would not be able to steal me back "in my four-year-old mind." I cannot explain to you how, but I understood every single word my mom spoke. Not in the literal context of the process itself and all the legal actions my parents had to go through, but that some other women carried me and gave me up. It was not a bad thing or a good thing. It just was.

As time went on, I learned of so many others on my block and in my family and friendship circles that were just like me: adopted. Chosen. Blessed by GOD to be here with loving parents who doted over our every move. This normalized adoption for me even more as a young child entering my tween years, not that I was looking for that or felt the need to be normalized. But like anything else knowing so many other children in my immediate circle were adopted gave me an additional sense of community. I do not think knowing this or not would have made me feel any differently about my family, it very well could have. But because there was never a lack of feeling loved and included, I will never know for sure. My family was all I knew at the time and based on what a four-year-old could measure in terms of happiness. I was incredibly happy.

A few years would pass, and my mom would periodically ask me if I had a desire to seek out my birth parents. My answer was always no. This went on up until my high school years. Figured she decided to stop asking because I was always so adamant there was no interest. This adoption has worked out very well for me in my opinion. It did not go without that small population that was aware of my adoption, who did not quite understand it in its totality and tried to make it ugly and shameful. Everyone just does not get the level of extraordinary that adoption makes you. Adoptees are CHOSEN. I was CHOSEN. For those attempting to or have attempted to make adoption negative, I challenge you to ask yourself the question? Are you certain that you were at the level of truly desired? Was everyone on the same page planning and anticipating your arrival with an overwhelming out-of-body type of joy? How much true preparation went into your arrival? What I know for sure is that my parents went through an entire process for me, and I am so happy they did.

Some of you are unknowingly guilty today of making adoption negative and shameful. If you have ever said, "They have three children, but that last child is their adopted child" this is where the educational moment happens. Making statements like this is inappropriate and unintentional or not causes a level of implied separation and inequality. If several children were naturally conceived and the parents go on to adopt a child and this happens more often than you think; all those children are equal. There is no difference and there should not be a difference. The process of adoption and the level of intent for parents seeking to have a baby is much like an addiction. It consumes them, it consumes their thoughts and drives their behaviors. The level of desire and intention a mother and father have that only having a child can fill. It is real. It dictates and impacts their daily lives from their thoughts, and fears and in some cases mimics desperation much like that of any other addiction or desire.

There are many definitions of adoption offered through search engines and hard copies of dictionaries. Adoption is also defined as "The act or process of giving official acceptance or approval to something." There is an entire process a potential parent must go through that includes multiple steps to even be considered to adopt, so it is a very intentional process. Depelchin Children's Center is one example where their adoption process has an entire life cycle that ranges from developing a family profile, conducting a home study, adoption plan creation, plans for moms and dads on both sides of the equation, and financial reviews to ensure that a family can properly care for a child with so much more in between. My point in sharing this information is to help everyone understand that there is more preparation and required preparedness that goes into the adoption process and that you should look at the adopted child no less than equal to children who were naturally conceived. Once a parent adopts that is their child. No doubt equal to all other children in the home. A few times I have just had to let people know; that I was chosen. My mama and daddy prepared for and sought me out. I was on the level of desired and wanted. Words are immensely powerful, and in all situations, you should be aware of your words how and to whom you deliver them, and most importantly what you are saying. They can change the trajectory of a life and there is a 50/50 chance that it could be positive or negative. Someone once said, your thoughts become your words, your words become your actions and your actions define your character and who you are as a human being. Stay positive it is important even when you are eyebrow-deep in negativity. One of the many important things my parents gave me was a solid foundation of self. Not things. Yes, I had a lot of things then and I have a lot of things now, but without them, I am still foundationally solid Michelle. For parents, this is a particularly important characteristic to teach your children.

CHAPTER TWO

MY WONDERFUL PARENTS WHO RAISED ME

As life would have it, I grew up with the best parents ever! My mother was a Corporate Diva, working for External Affairs in a large company named Southwestern Bell Telephone Company, some of you know it today as AT&T. She grew up in Fifth Ward, Texas, and would let you know that every opportunity she could. The only girl of four siblings, she had a nice upbringing. She was firm, graceful, beautiful, and a class act; some would even say she was regal. Had the best sense of humor and loved life. Seeking out new experiences and learning new things was always exciting to her. At 5ft 9in and a solid size 12-14 with a narrow 9AA, sometimes AAA foot, she was my hero. Never once tried to justify the cost or explain her choices. That was who she was as a person. Every day and I mean every day she would get up and get dressed to the nines, make-up, and all. On several of those days, she had nowhere to go but she stayed ready. She and her besties had the best fun. I would love to see them interact with each other and the stories they would tell. During her career, she must have partnered with every woman and minority-owned business in the city of

Houston and the entire state of Texas in the 1980s and early 1990s. As far back as I can remember I was right there with her all dolled up attending lunch, brunch, dinner, or some banquet one after another. During my younger years, I participated in ballet, baton, and tap-dancing classes. Tap dance was my least favorite, but dancing made my heart happy. My mother exposed me to everything under the sun from her career experiences and hobbies as she served as my number one role model and demonstrated an excellent work ethic. If she said it once, she said it a thousand times. Michelle, you need to make sure that you can take care of yourself and your children when you have them, even if you get married. She would say men change and they can stay, or they can go, but you should always be prepared to take care of yourself and your children. Go to college and get yourself a Business Degree this way you can do anything you want professionally. As I reflect it was like a mantra, she said it that often. In my case, it turns out she was right.

My father was a Plant Supervisor at Uncle Ben's Rice. He worked for The Mar's Corporation for 32 years before retiring. He mastered shift work so there were some weeks I would not see him because of the hours. Back then he would be off for two days between shift changes. But on those days that he was off we would ride around in our family van for what seemed like hours in my young eyes. I would have my Coca Cola and he would have his beer. By today's standards this would not be a good look, but do not judge. My dad was 5ft 9in and it was cute to me that he and my mom were the same height, and she would be a tad bit taller than him when she wore heels. If you knew my dad then and you know him now, you are aware that he will say anything to you or about you right to your face. And everyone loves him unconditionally no matter what comes out of his mouth. Back to the Coca-Cola and beer, keep in mind we also did not have seatbelt requirements and you could ride a bike and skateboard without a helmet and knee pads too. But back to the story at hand. It would seem as though we were riding all day in my eyes as a little girl and now that I am older, I realize it was only one neighborhood over from where we lived.

Turns out my parents started early creating a family and gave birth to my older brother Cedric during their high school years. My parents met incredibly young, in high school as the story goes. They met at a wedding of a dear friend of my mother's and a cousin of my dad. Fast forward my mom became pregnant with my brother; gave birth and three years later she and my dad got married. It was a beautiful ceremony at her parent's, my maternal grandparents' house. Both of my parents attended Texas Southern University in Houston, Texas. One of the many Historically Black Colleges and Universities referred to as HBCU's today. During this time, they attended school and worked while raising my brother. Looking back there was always some level of inner family rivalry. North Forest was the best school district ever during this time and you cannot tell those that matriculated through that district anything different thirty-plus years later. My brother attended and graduated from Forest Brook High School, and I attended and graduated from M.B. Smiley High School. These were the rivals of all rivals during this time. We lived for the night these two schools played football, so we could argue over who had the best team and band in the nation. And that would be M.B. Smiley of course! The rivalry continued when I decided to go to The Prairie View A&M University where The Marching Storm was the best band in the land. And yours truly was a Black Fox, band royalty, and kept that fifty-yard line on fire back in the day.

I may have previously mentioned that my older brother and I are ten years apart. Being the spoiled little sister, I followed him everywhere and he took me everywhere else I did not follow. Bike rides for us were the best especially when dogs would chase us. My brother had a 10-speed bike back then and I spent many days on those handlebars as we rode through our neighborhood. If we were not riding bikes, then I was at his band practice or some other after-school activity during his high school years. Because of the huge gap in our ages, I knew so many of his classmates and their families. If you were not in the know as to how I came to join this wonderful family, you would have never questioned my existence I fit in so well.

My parents were always transparent about the adoption. It was never a secret and was never presented or thought about as negative. It was not thought about or discussed hardly ever once we had the initial conversation, aside from the periodic inquiry as to whether I wanted to seek out my birth parents. I was blessed to grow up in a loving home and was spoiled beyond one's imagination and again how I got there was never a thought. Mama and daddy were mama and daddy, and I knew nothing else. Early morning house cleaning and watching Soul Train was a Saturday morning highlight number. It was not until I got to college that I realized everyone did not come from a two-parent home and that the family dynamic had a lot of different combinations. Growing up I cannot ever remember going to a house, where there was not a mom and dad or both grandparents that served as guardians. During this era, as kids, we loved to go to school so we could dress up in our finest fashions. I can remember my mother saying I need you to make up your mind little girl. Last week it was bell bottoms that had to cover your shoes, now this week it's straight legs. Oh, and let us not forget Gloria Vanderbilt's famous tight jeans with the slit at the ankle, my all-time favorite and I had to have them in every color available. Along with going to the corner 7-Eleven for that Icee, chips and Now and Later candy life was wonderful. Our generation was a bit more advanced in my opinion than kids today. I never remembered my mom having to organize my clothes for the week, pack my lunch, or do any of those things. We were an all-American family. Not perfect by any means, but there was no shortage of discipline, love, and admiration in our home.

My parents traveled a lot for pleasure. Every time I looked up, they were going on a cruise or to what in my mind sounded like some cool place. Once I made it to middle school I spoke up and said those days were over. They could not go anymore unless they took me. And just like that, I started going on vacation every year. From New York, Los Angeles, San Francisco, and Hawaii, cruises to the Bahamas and so many more wonderful places in between. I was living the life and wishing I had spoken up earlier. The two trips that stand out the most to me were my first-time visiting Manhattan, NY. We stayed at what back then was the Barbizon Hotel on 140 E and 63rd Street across from Central Park. This was a fancy place with doormen that stood outside the entrance and held the doors open for you as your entered. My Uncle Clarence, by way of my God Mother Martha Ann, and his wife lived there, and boy did they love to entertain. May they all rest in peace and will forever live in my memories. Every day we were picked up by a limousine and taken on tours of the city. We shopped at the famous Bloomingdale's and all up and down 5th Avenue just about every day we were there. Bloomingdales was where I saw Isabel Sanford from one of my favorite sitcoms The Jefferson's and Phil Donahue of the Phil Donahue Show shopping there as though it was any other day, and no one bothered them which was even more amazing to me. We had dinner at the Windows of the World Restaurant, located at what was then the World Trade Center in the North Tower. On the 106th and 107th floors, you could see the breathtaking scenery of Manhattan, NY in every direction as the hustle and bustle of weight staff who tended to our every whim filled the room along with the chatter of others enjoying dinner with friends and family. Having visited as a child witnessing the events of 911 as an adult was emotional for everyone who witnessed and lived through it, but it was especially sad for me because I had been there and knew what it was like riding up that elevator 106 floors feeling as though it took an eternity. The slow ride up allowed you to feel the transitions every so often and like most tall buildings for security purposes, we had to get off every so often on a different floor and change elevators to get to the next few levels. The slowest and longest elevator ride of my entire life and I am so grateful to have had the experience. Having firsthand knowledge of what those people trapped on those floors could have possibly felt on 911 having been there was overwhelming knowing the landscape. Other memories of this trip included us riding through Harlem in the limo and people swarming the car and hitting the windows desperately trying to see who was inside was the first time I felt threatened during the entire trip, and I just wanted to get back to the hotel. Once my Uncle Clarence let the window down and spoke, they all just backed away from the car. I remember thinking to myself what did he say that I did not hear that resulted in such calm? Now that I am an adult, I honestly believe it was the fact that he was a black man in a limo signaling a sign of success to the masses surrounding the car; he was someone in their community who made it and this was an unspoken language people of color have used for years. Hence, it made it okay for him to be there. The second trip was to Hawaii. The fanfare upon arrival was unlike any I had ever experienced. Waikiki, Honolulu was just too much for me though, it could have been the timing of the 4th of July weekend and it felt like I just as well had been in the crowded streets of New York City, NY. The only difference was I had never seen so many people with picture-perfect bodies walking around in very skimpy swimwear in large numbers and not necessarily on the beach. We stayed in condos allowing you to walk out the back sliding door and you were just a few feet from the Pacific Ocean. Experiencing my first real luau was amazing and Hawaii is breathtaking. Those over-the-top performances by the dancers and their colorful costumes were beautiful. To see the preparation of that pig as it is lowered into a pit in the ground to be cooked for what we would later enjoy as dinner was so interesting to witness.

I always had a voice and knew when to use it and equally when not. From every indicator that meant something to me.

I never felt like anything other than this was my family and how life was supposed to be because it was all I knew. All I ever felt was love and adoration from my parents and extended family.

My maternal grandparents lived near us in the neighborhood just three short miles away and I spent a lot of time with them growing up. This is where I would go after school both in elementary and middle school. It was so close; I could walk to and from school every day. Especially when my mother had late evening work engagements that I could not attend due to scheduling conflicts. My maternal grandmother, Mae Etta was the best. She had a garden in the backyard and liked to cook using fresh vegetables and making things from scratch. I do not doubt that growing up watching her and how she did things in the kitchen, influenced my enjoyment of cooking and entertaining to this day. Her meals were like gourmet-level soul food dishes we now pay top dollar for in boutique restaurants. On any given day we would pick collard greens and herbs out of the backyard garden and pair them with short ribs or a pot roast. No one can convince me that Luby's did not steal her liver and onions recipe. When I say hers tasted exactly like theirs believe me it did. She was a housewife and periodically did some work outside of the home after raising her four children. She just moved me right on in and took care of me and some of my cousins that would visit from time to time while our parents worked. I cannot ever remember a day or night while staying at my grandparents' house when I did not have breakfast, lunch, a snack, supper, and dinner. We went to church every time the doors opened. To be clear we were there for Sunday school, Sunday service, Choir Rehearsal, Mission Meeting, Deacon Meeting, and Prayer Meeting every single week. Those Mission ladies in all-white dresses with matching white hats scared me to my very core. Especially when they put that white glove at your mouth if you were caught chewing gum in church. A peppermint was as far as you could go back then but after church, you could have gum. Remember the original packs of Wrigley's Spearmint gum? One of the sweet church ladies offered me a piece of gum and of course asked my grandmother if it was okay for me to have a piece. She went into her purse pulled out a stick of gum and gave me half of a gum stick. I graciously said thank you and we left out of the church. When we made it to the car my grandmother was furious! She said she could have kept that little half-stick of gum. "You deserve a whole stick of gum or do not give you a damn thing." It was so funny to me, but she was big mad, and I think that was the first time I heard her curse, and we were still in the church parking lot. Fussing underneath her breath in the car all the way home. Periodically, I would hear, 'my grandbaby deserves a whole stick of gum.'

All such wonderful memories. I spent a lot of time with my maternal grandmother and when she died, a part of me died with her. As a young child, I was not shielded from death. It was important back then that family members were able to transition at home with their families by their side. My first experience with death was with my Great Grandmother Idella. She was my grandfather's mother. I remember vividly being at the house and she was laying on the couch with a blanket covering her. She kept asking for my grandfather who was at that time rushing to the house from work. He walked in the door, she said come hold my hand and he did. Once he took her hand, she said I love you and took her last breath. That was my very first hands-on experience with death. My grandmother, like my mom, was my everything, and just knowing that death was so final was life-changing for me then as a young teen at the time of my grandmother's death. My maternal grandmother passed before my high school graduation, and I remember wanting her to be there so badly. But I found joy in the thought that she was in heaven smiling down on me as I walked across that stage to receive my high school diploma. Just to think that the more things change the more they stay the same is mind-boggling sometimes. What I mean by this is that as my mother was preparing for her mother my grandmother's funeral, she was also planning a graduation party for me. Fast forward 25 plus years when my mother passed, I was planning her funeral while planning my daughter's birthday celebration, which happened to fall on the same day we laid my mother to rest in what was her final resting place. It was truly a day of celebrating life. The range of emotions and numbness of going through that season. I am still amazed that I made it through and remained sane. There are situations in life when you recognize your mental and internal strengths. No doubt this season was one for me. Although I was never shielded from death. My involvement in the planning and arrangements never became a reality until my mother's passing.

My maternal grandfather worked at the Post Office where he retired after many years of service. He was a wonderful provider to my grandmother and their family, and he took care of her until she passed, and my dad did the same for my mother. What I can say about both my dad and my maternal grandfather, no matter their faults and shortcomings are that the women in their lives did not go without anything their hearts desired and were provided for beyond their wildest imagination. Talk about a King taking care of his Queen, they were true examples of that in every measurable detail. My paternal grandparents were not around as much. I would see them periodically mostly on holidays, but I knew who they were and again George and Cassie showed me nothing but love and acceptance.

CHAPTER THREE

NEW LESSONS, UNEXPECTED CHANGES

As I got older when my parents and I would go places, I recall people would make references to how much I looked like my mom and dad, whether we were all together or I was with one or the other. And we would just laugh as though it was our inside joke. It was not a secret, and we never felt the need to explain it. My mother showed up with a baby out of nowhere and it was certainly not a secret. Everyone around me for the most part knew, but there was not a lot of talk about it or asking questions. Again, it was not a good thing or a bad thing it just was.

Then the tides turned a bit, and my perfect home began to look and feel different. Out of nowhere, my brother became a little rebellious, to say the least. We came home one day from one of my dance recitals to find a note on the coffee table saying he was leaving home and never coming back. My mother found the note and read it out loud to me and my dad as we stood in the middle of the family room in total disbelief. As my mother read the letter it was incomprehensible to me. Once again that I could remember in this life second only to the passing of my maternal grandmother I was devastated and speechless. Where could he be? Why would he leave? I just never understood it and it made me so sad. As I reflect on that moment, I learned how gangster my mother was when she said, how is a grown-ass man running away? He should be gone. That is what you do leave your parent's house when you turn eighteen. That stuck with me forever. I knew that once I grew up and turned eighteen, I had to leave my parents' house. As I am processing this new lesson, she balled up the letter threw it in the trash, and went on as if nothing had ever happened. My dad and I continued to stand there watching her but never said a word. And it was that very moment where you knew you had better not ask any questions or make a comment. It was complete silence for what felt like hours. But it was immediate that I missed my brother so much. The days turned into weeks and the weeks turned into months. The months turned into years, where I worried about how his life was progressing, where was he, and the unanswered question, why did he leave? I was in the fifth grade around this time so with him leaving it instantly changed to me pretty much being the only child. We did not talk about my brother much during this season. He left and according to my parents he was supposed to leave at that age and life just kept moving. And like most things in life, we adjust to our new normal desired or not, and just kept moving forward. Continued to create memories together. Special memories that my brother missed out on and for no reason that I can intelligently sum up today. I do not believe that there is a connection between my adoption and why my brother abruptly left the house to take on the world alone. I think to this day he just wanted to be his own person and make his own decisions. It was a sad time for me because at that young age as mature as I was the pieces of the puzzle just did not fit. But as life would have it time passes, and you adjust to change. My brother and I have not spoken in a little over three years now by his own choice and I am okay with his choice, and I respect that choice. As adults, you are entitled to make the decisions that you feel are best for you.

Like all families there were imperfections. It was not always sunshine, rainbows, and rose-colored glasses. There were disagreements about small and sometimes big things. There were financial difficulties and infidelity. All lessons were not delivered via conversations and there were a lot of those. Most times it was delivered by way of examples of behaviors that would shift from heartbreak and sadness to happiness and the cycle would repeat itself. And then to quiet days where no words were spoken, and body language could resemble brokenness to outward gestures that begged for forgiveness. No matter what forgiveness and love always found a way to prevail.

As a family, we celebrated holidays, birthdays, weddings, and graduations of family and friends and continued to travel. During this time, we were now joined by one less person when my brother left. As the years continued to pass and I became more involved in extracurricular activities and the travel requirements increased as I graduated from high school and moved on to college. My parents attended every dance recital, concert performance, and half-time football game performance from grade school and throughout my college years. Location was never a factor, and it did not matter where those games were my parents were there with bells on to support me. Not only were they there for me they also traveled with my cousin Troy who grew to become more like a big brother to me and still is to this day. Troy was a star athlete at Madison High School and I attended what was known at that time as M.B. Smiley High School, home of the Mighty Golden Eagles both located in Houston, Texas. Friday night lights were a real thing back then just as it is today. High School football was everything. As previously mentioned, Saturday morning house cleaning and watching Soul Train was highlight number one. We were not overwhelmed with social media and negative news day in and day out as this current generation is suffering through. I liked that we would not learn about the news until the next day and sometimes weeks later. Kids today do not understand the complexities of what they are losing and have lost tied to a computer screen day in and day out.

My college life was my first real glimpse into how different the family dynamic looked in other homes. As I made new friends who were from all over the country it was clear that my parents kept me in a bubble. I say this because as I learned then and it still holds even today families look different and are made up of non-traditional dynamics. Some of my new friends came from homes where their siblings, aunts, uncles, or grandparents raised them. Some did not have a mother or father in the picture. And like adoption today that family dynamic has evolved. You can have a single mother, a single father, two moms, or two dads. It is my wholehearted belief that all who seek adoption to expand a family unit should continue to do so as often as they can if it is financially feasible. To care for and unconditionally love a child is changing lives for the better and I am hopeful that this path continues for many years to come. I am so grateful for my journey and experience. If there is a regret for me today it is that I never went through with the process to adopt a child and give that gift of unconditional love. Although it is not quite the same, I love my extended family's children as though they are mine and I try to support and encourage, celebrate and lift them as if they are mine.

Before meeting my husband, getting engaged, and ultimately getting married I made the decision that I wanted to adopt. I wanted my daughter to have a brother and it was as simple as making a phone call to Depelchin Children's Center to inquire about the process and start my journey of adopting a son as a single mother. I wanted an older child eight years old or older. A newborn was just not an option. As a blended family, my husband's children were adults. His baby girl was a teenager when we met, and my only daughter Neely Simone was wrapping up middle school and about to be a freshman in high school. Apart from me feeling bad about having my husband start over again I was no longer able to naturally have children, not that this would have been an option for me. My experience with pregnancy was tough so it was not an experience that I was excited about having again. Once my husband Reginald and I talked about it he was open to adoption the obstacle before us is he wanted a baby which to me defeated my purpose. Most parents who adopt are looking for newborns and not older children and that was my focus. As time passed and we were not agreeable to proceed that dream faded and I tucked that desire away and moved on. We were also so close to being empty nesters and I just never pushed the issue. I just wanted to give another child the blessing that was afforded me through the adoption process. The greatest gift of all from this experience is being taught by two of the best human beings to ever be on this side of heaven to enjoy life to the fullest and help other people along the way.

My parents and I celebrated with each other daily. We used fine China all the time and it did not have to be for a special occasion or holiday. It could have been used on any day for something as simple as a hamburger and chips. And we always invited others to share our meals and joy with us. There was no shortage of love and discipline in our household. If you did something wrong, you were guaranteed to be corrected and or punished as necessary. If I brought you home, you were instantly treated like family welcomed, and knew you had to follow the rules of the house. I am proud to say that my household today replicates that example.

There were so many important lessons learned growing up by watching these two amazing human beings whom I called mom and dad. Starting with there was nothing too difficult to overcome. They both demonstrated a strong work ethic, and my father was very entrepreneurial. We always had a side business of some sort. My dad did real estate and had a record shop in the '70s when music was at its best and his last venture was a Limousine Service. They taught me to look at every opportunity and learn from it along with living and experiencing life to the fullest. But made it clear that there was a lot of hard work required on the front end. As my mom drilled this same message into me, I continue to say those same words to my daughter today. "No matter your situation married or not always be able to take care of yourself and your children. Go to college and get your business degree that way you can go into any profession and industry and be successful. It is better to have a degree and not need it than to need a degree and not have it, especially for you baby girl. The world unfortunately is still not color blind and sometimes gender will play a role in decision-making as well. You will be refused or denied opportunities based on the hue of your skin. It is a systemic issue that we are still attempting to rectify today. My mother must have said that to me a million times. However, unlike me, she never gave a specific example of her experience. I was able to give Neely examples of my personal experiences so that she could see and understand that her mother had hills to climb and battles to fight. Sometimes I came out on the winning side and sometimes I did not. Continuing to move forward and learn from life's disappointments and shortfalls continue to set yourself up to advance and help others along the way. Treating others with the same respect you would like in return and demanding it in situations where it is not always freely extended were a few of the biggest takeaways from my parents. All failures should be manifested into learning tools to immediately or over time become success stories. If you want something in life the word no or denied always means delayed until that yes arrives.

Chapter Four

The Phone Call After, The Phone Call

It was a bright sunny day and I had just arrived at the park for my daily walk. During this time in my life, I was obsessed with losing weight and being fit. Every day during this season I would work out at the gym during my lunch hour and after work. I was introduced to Memorial Park and would make my way around at least once to satisfy that 3.5 miles. It felt good to be outside and around people with like-minded health conscience goals. Apart from those moms who would lap me with one sometimes two babies in a stroller with the family dog on a leash, it was all bliss. Seeing that truly rocks your insecurities and further defined why I needed to be there. Back then just making it around once was the goal and I struggled to get it done every day. The weekends were no exception. In between sorority meetings and required committee meetings I would walk at the park just to make sure I got in a workout every single day. Somehow, I found the will to push through just to maintain.

On this day, the park was full of healthy conscience very fit people and then there was me inspired by them and I did not know any of them. Typical Houston kind of hot sunny day and my cell phone rang just as I was getting out of the car. Is this Michelle? Yes, I replied to the unfamiliar voice on the other end of the line. This is Kelley the Case Worker calling you from Depelchin Children's Center regarding your inquiry. I do not have a lot of information for you right now, but I do have a few questions. Do you know if you had or have a twin sister? The reason I ask is that there is a file with similar information, but the dates are off by two years, and I am wondering if that is a typo or not. My response back to her was "I better not have a twin and Michael and Betty do not know about it" laughing to myself, but so serious at the same time. She said let me do some additional investigating and I will give you a callback. It will be at least a week or two before you should look to hear back from me. I replied, I cannot wait to see where this goes, and I hung up the cell phone and I hit the trail as though it was any other day. Intrigued by the thought that I could have a twin. And recalling all those times that I have been asked if I had a twin. It was so frequent that I thought it was the latest pick-up line from guys trying to get my number. And a couple of times it worked!

A few days passed and the phone rings again and it was the caseworker, Kelley. I have some additional information for you. Me surprised and curious for the first time that I could recall. Do I have a twin? What did you find? I asked with great anticipation. She proceeded to say I shared with you that there was another file that was quite like yours. It turns out the information is the same and you may have been the missing link for several years that brought this all together. What do you mean I asked? Well, I can share with you that you have a biological sister, and she too was given up for adoption through us as well and that is why the files were so similar. Wait! What? It took some time to digest that I have a sister and she was also given up for adoption two years after me. Kelley went on to say you have the same mother for certain however, I cannot verify anything on the paternal side as the identity of the father is not clear on either file. As recent as 1992 the sister reached out to us trying to make a connection and left a profile with her personal information along with a contact phone number. The last time the mother reached out was in 1988 and she too left a personal profile with contact information as well. What will have to happen from here is that I will reach out to validate if the information is still current and to see where they are and if there is still interest in connecting. Once I contact both of them I will call you back and let you know the next steps, providing there are next steps. This information is dated so it may not be valid. Okay! I replied but I was completely overwhelmed by this information. So much so that I had to just stop and sit and process what she had just said. Forcing myself to think simple enough I will just wait to hear back. This was, however, far from simple. There was never a thought that this road could lead to a sibling.

Now there was an odd nervousness that set in, and it was fear. My mind began to race with the what-if questions again. I have a sister. What if they have changed their minds about connecting? What if it is someone I already know? Wonder if we look alike? And these questions swirled in my head on and on for what seemed like hours. And the wait was not a long one at all to get the answers to every question. Maybe a week or so passed and here I was again talking to the Case Manager. She was able to reach my biological sister and it turns out she was agreeable to speak to and meet me. I reflect again, here I am on a journey to find my birth mother and instead find a biological sister who was also given up for adoption. What are the odds of that happening? Talk about a curveball that was just not anticipated or even a possibility in my mind. I have no idea what to do with this now that it is here and very much in my face. But I agreed to move forward, and an introduction phone call was immediately scheduled. Within twenty-four hours I was on the phone talking to a total stranger who was my biological sister, and her name was Danielle.

Danielle and I sounded alike and had the same crazy laugh, and it was as though we had known each other all our lives the connection was so instant. As we began to talk and share according to her, we lived in the same general area and were not far apart geographically at all. It was scary to me that we were within ten short miles of each other and had been for at least five years. It took zero time for us to agree to meet. After our initial phone call, we both gave the agency the thumbs up to schedule a meeting. It took no time for confirmation to arrive.

The day has arrived, and Danielle and I are scheduled to meet later this evening. It was a beautiful sunny day and during this time I was so conservative and corporate. It was not a thought for me to throw on a designer suit and go! Now, which designer was the question? Should I go dark? Should I add color to not come across as drab and dark? Reminding myself that this is not a professional interview or presentation. After going back and forth and realizing that I had gone through this entire journey alone up until this point. No one aside from my mom and dad was aware that I had started this journey, not a line sister, another Soror, family member, or friend. I had not told one person to bounce these questions off or to give me an opinion on what to wear or how I should approach this situation now that I am eyebrow deep and continue to move forward. My parents were probably just as nervous and anxious as I was as we moved through this process. I lived in the Galleria area at the time and the drive time to our meeting location was short. My parents were meeting me there, so I guess I was not alone. My stomach was in knots and the palms of my hands were sweaty as I drove to the center. My mind was racing wondering how this was going to go. What do I say? What will she look like? Do we look alike? What if it's someone I already know? Do we hug or shake hands? Is she a hugger? Will I cry? Jesus, please do not have me in here crying like a baby! We have spoken previously so there is some familiarity between us. It will not be a first-time interaction.

I had so many unanswered questions leading up to this point. Wondering how she felt about being put up for adoption and how she felt now knowing I too was given up for adoption? Will this commonality make us close? Will we have a bond like no other due to our journey? I was trying to process all of this as well and just could not quite grasp the reality that the time was here. It was heavy and I was extremely nervous about the meeting. I had never been to Depelchin Children's Center before that day as an adult that I could remember. But I had an idea of the general location based on the address. Upon arrival, the building was very pretty and I was sure that there had been many upgrades and expansions to the building since I had been there as a newborn almost thirty years prior. As I sat in the parking lot my mind flashed back to the countless times that I had passed by this building. I looked at it and admired its beauty and never truly realized how great a role this very structure played in my life.

Here we are now! The agency has arranged the initial in-person meeting between Danielle and me and it is now in motion within a few minutes we would finally meet face to face. Immediately upon her walking into that room where I sat and awaited her arrival. I immediately saw that there was a resemblance and we hit it off just like that and there were no surprises there. Just reflecting on the many conversations, we shared over the phone. Back then there were details that I just did not think about and when I showed up empty-handed, she presented me with a beautiful bouquet of flowers. As I hugged her, I thanked her for agreeing to meet me and for the flowers. All I could think to myself is

Michelle you are a total loser right now. No idea why but I did. How could I have not thought about bringing her flowers? Danielle was super sweet and our first meeting was one that I would describe as a beautiful experience.

Both of our families were incredibly supportive. My parents were with me during this meeting and so was Danielle's husband at the time. He was a genuinely nice guy and incredibly attentive to her. There was an age difference, but you could see and feel the mutual love between the two. In my mind, I am thinking we both like older men yay!! I get it Sis, and this was so my inside joke that will be saved for another book. We sat and talked in that room for what seemed like hours. It was as though we had known each other forever. Everyone was so calm and casual and it was not a hard meeting at all. The case manager applauded us on how seamless our meeting came together but felt the need to remind us that this was a miracle of sorts because for so many this is not the outcome. She reminded us that we may have to do this again with our biological mother. And that it may or may not be as easy or it may not happen at all. And just like that all over again it felt as though a ton of rocks hitting me on the head because I realized she was right. The very thought of this meeting between my birth mother and I would not happen never entered my mind. The Case Manager went on to say it may not be this easy. Selfishly, I thought to myself I have so many questions primarily about my health history, so this meeting must happen. Most would think that one's thought process in situations like this is focused on the million-dollar question:' why you were given up for adoption in the first place.' And I was not at all concerned about why my birth mother gave me up and that may be hard for some to believe or digest. It is such a no-brainer; it must be the why behind anyone seeking to find their birth parents. Yet, my focus to that date was strictly centered around health concerns. What should I be knowledgeable of so I can share this information with my doctors? Meeting both my biological sister and my mother of course is and was a true bonus no doubt and a substantial win for all of us. A moment I will never and would never take for granted. It just was not the driver behind the action that propelled me to this point. Meeting them was a wonderful, beautiful experience, and as I reflect on and write this book. I am prayerful that others will be so lucky as to get this far and just meet your biological family if there is a desire to take this journey.

The question that came up often the older I got was details about my family health history. I am that person that goes to the doctor every year like clockwork to get my annual exams and blood work done. If anything seems off short of a broken fingernail, I was at the doctor's office. So as the years continue to pass you can recall every time you go to the doctor. There is that one piece of paper. The one where you are asked to complete the health questionnaire. The page where it lists the column for your mother and a column for your father. Under each of these columns, there is a host of possible health conditions that could exist on both sides of the family. If I never thought about the fact that I was adopted and if the conversation of adoption never reared its head this was always the time it would creep up. And not knowing began to cause real issues for me. The not knowing and not having a clue as to where to begin to find the answers became unsettling. If you are adopted and have never met your biological family, there is no doubt in my mind that you can relate to this very example. This annual experience and every single time I would go to a new doctor because my insurance carrier changed, the annual update, or I needed to see a Specialist. It all reminded me that there was a piece of the puzzle that was missing. A piece of my life puzzle that was missing and I needed those pieces to put it all together.

In my mind, she must still be interested. Selfish as it was, she just had to be agreeable to meet because I needed to know some things that only she could answer. It was genuinely nice and exciting to learn about and meet my biological sister, extremely enjoyable. Now that she is a part of my life it was a bonus that I could not have anticipated when I began to seek out my biological mother. And I can echo that today because we still talk and continue to keep in touch. But at that moment and on that day, I had questions that only my biological mother could answer. And I immediately shifted back to the why behind my actions.

CHAPTER FIVE

A LOOK BACK APPROXIMATELY THREE MONTHS PRIOR

My job at the time sent me to a conference in Dallas, Texas. It was my first technology conference, and I was excited about the opportunity to expand my knowledge in the field and the official leadership had made such a big deal about it. So, we are finally on day three of the conference and it is the closing mixer. While standing at the bar with a guy I met from a local company who was also in attendance at the conference and who was as ready as I was to go home. We are casually chatting about the conference and the information we learned in the many sessions we attended. As we are talking, we noticed people getting up from a table beet red or super pale and heading straight to the bar right next to us. It was so funny because one after another and another they would rise from that table where an exceedingly small lady sat across from them and would run to the bar for a drink pretty much all shots of Tequila or the shot of choice. Andre was his name and the name of the company he worked for escaped me. He turned to me and said, whatever that lady is saying to them I have absolutely no interest and I echoed his sentiments as well. Thought to myself neither do I and this is insane yet quite comical to watch. The night continued and before I knew it my leadership team was hammered and had become the life of the party. As I looked around the room a feeling of gratefulness gave me comfort. The room had thinned out a bit, but to my shock, my name is being called very loudly, and ever so slowly my body and eyes slowly turn around to look in that direction. Come over here my boss yells across the room. Super embarrassed I excused myself and made my way over to the rest of the team. Have a seat and get your palm read. No doubt my expression was that of a cartoon character as my eyes pretty much bulged out of my head. WHAT? Not in my inside voice either. Sit down get your palm read she repeated laughing as it was so entertainingly funny for her. Went on to introduce the lady sitting across the table as though they were long-lost friends. This is a Clairvoyant, and she reads palms. Being polite with zero doubts my facial expression was saying what in the whole hell? As my eyes locked with the lady the words hello uttered out of my mouth ever so quietly. Somehow the strength to make that happen just showed up. My mind on the other hand was on a different track equal to where is the closest exit. Quickly and politely extended a thank you but no thanks I am good. Certain this would put an end to the foolery witnessed at that moment. And then the peer pressure came from the entire group who were super drunk, do it, do it, do it! So, to stop them from chanting I took a seat. Immediately told the lady on the other side of the table, I only believe in GOD, I do not believe in any of this stuff, and I am only participating because as you can see, I have no choice.

She looks at me and smiles. Says her gift is a gift from GOD. In my head, I am 'like whatever lady at the same time saying fix your face, Michelle.' Something I felt I had been saying most of the night as the foolishness continued to compound. She then asks for my palms, and I reluctantly gave them to her. She turned them over and said you are not from here. Immediately responding, no Houston is home. She then says you do not like your current employment situation. Before the word 'no' could form, she responded, 'no worries it will get better.' That made me laugh but anyone with a pulse would have figured that out just looking at the distance I purposefully maintain all evening. She goes on to say you have lots of siblings. No ma'am thinking to myself here is the fraud peeking its head out. Just one sibling I said boldly. She immediately followed up with no you have lots of siblings. I am showing you to have lots of siblings. In my mind side-eyeing her with lips tooted to the ceiling still thinking you are the fraud I thought you are and as I opened my mouth to say, lady, I only have one brother. Stopped mid-word not mid-sentence but mid-word. At that moment it dawned on me that she could be right. There is a real chance that lots of siblings could very well exist. Aside from doctors' visits, it was the first time in years that I felt that it does exist, and again here it is saying hey Michelle! It is some more people out there that you are related to ma'am. At that moment, aside from the doctor visits, I could only think of one other time my adoption was a thing. The day of my college graduation from Prairie View A&M University like all the other years past was on Mother's Day weekend. My entire family, parents, aunts, uncles, cousins, and a host of friends and extended family were all there cheering me on and celebrating me. This was a huge and awesome accomplishment. Soaking it all in walking across that stage to accept my diploma and then standing to take that picture commemorating the experience. As I could hear my name being yelled from the stands walking back to my seat. I looked around the baby dome at all the attendees for this amazing ceremonious occasion and thought to myself; I wonder if my biological mother would be proud to know that I graduated from college? What joy would she have knowing she made the right decision? Would she be proud, not just of me but for her wisdom and strength? Fleeting though it was but a thought, nonetheless. Aside from the doctor visits, and my college graduation day, the Clairvoyant was yet another time I could recall wondering who are my biological parents.

This Clairvoyant went on to ask me if I was living with someone. Immediately, I said no. She said it appears that you are seeing someone, and he is profoundly serious about you. He is contemplating marriage. She went on to say that she knew that my parents were not on board with this relationship, and they were not but things would get better and that I should not worry. She shuffled some cards and looked at my palms some more. Then she said, you are going to get diamonds. Lots of them and one will be an engagement ring. I laughed out loud and immediately jumped back to this woman who has no clue what she is talking about. She went further to say you will get an engagement ring in June. Laughing out loud this time again because in my mind getting married was nowhere near a possibility. That was not a thought, short-term or long-term goal for me. My decision to call it quits was firm upon my return home from this trip.

Deciding to let the cat out of the bag. The perfect time arrived for me to tell the Clairvoyant about my adoption at birth. And that was the one time I think she gave me that look I had been giving her all night; that "heifer I know you are adopted" look. Do not for one minute think you are telling me something I do not already know. Sitting here telling you that you have a lot of siblings all evening and I know you do not know any of them. Yet again, very politely she said yes, and you have lots of siblings. She cursed me in her head, no way she did not. I was wearing her out in my head, so I know we were both going there. We proceeded with the session. What blew me away was when she said, you will meet them along with your entire biological family and it will be a good meeting. Shock, disbelief, the mecca of how that will happen just rained down on my head. No time to ask the question, the drunk work crew returned, and we talked a bit more before calling it a night. Nothing was of significance as we had an audience. I did not share anything I was told by the Clairvoyant with my team. I just said it was okay and I was going to turn it in for the night. During that night I could not reconcile the comment that I would meet my biological family. All these years have passed and reflecting on the countless times my mother would ask me if

I wanted to pursue meeting them or seek them out and every time, I said no and felt with no uncertainty that I meant no.

The conference is now over, and I grabbed a quick breakfast before heading to the airport excited about going back home. I never thought anything else about the reading, the information the Clairvoyant shared, or anything. My belief was very much still that all of what she said was not true. Made it home the next day and jumped right back into my routine. Went to visit my parents and we had Sunday dinner as usual, and all felt well. After dinner, my mom and I would retire upstairs to the guest bedroom where we kept the family computer. That computer almost got my mother in a ton of trouble. Here I am starting my career and both of my parents were retired and had been retired since I left for college. Her thing after retirement was interior design and computer technology. She was the computer queen and software engineer of the family. I would get to work and have thirty emails in my inbox, and I would think to myself, what happened overnight that I have thirty emails? All thirty emails would have been from my mother and all of them would be chain emails. I finally had to tell her that if she did not stop sending me these chain emails, I was going to be forced to block her. But it was this very computer that almost got her blocked that we would retire to after Sunday dinner. As I sat there playing Solitaire on the computer our game of choice, we would just be chatting up a storm as always. Out of nowhere she jumps up and says I almost forgot I have a diamond ring I have been meaning to give you. You would have thought she said she was going to shoot me in the head. I yelled out what diamond ring? Body language as though I was clutching my invisible pearls. She looked at me so puzzled. Why are you acting so crazy, and I am about to give you diamonds? I said you just took me by surprise, and I was not expecting this is all. She leaves the room and comes back with a ring that I had been eyeing in her jewelry box for years. She gives it to me and says it just needs to be cleaned but I am tired of it and plan to get another one so you can have this one. Of course, with a big grin on my face admiring it on my finger I said thank you! Then I began to tell her about my experience with the Clairvoyant to help her understand my initial reaction and she was all ears. It was the best girls' gossip session ever. She was so entertained by what I experienced and after every detail, she was quick to follow up with what else did she say? I told my mom everything from start to finish and how insane the experience was for me. We laughed together and joked about it and moved on to other topics as though it was a story about someone else's life. And it did feel like it was someone else's life. That was how transparent we were all the time about everything. I stayed for a few more hours and then headed home.

Then fast forward a few months later out of nowhere one morning in early May of that same year, I woke up from my sleep with this overwhelming feeling. It was so powerful that I was moved to jump into action and start looking up numbers and making phone calls to no one other than Depelchin Children's Center. I knew from my mother that Depelchin handled my adoption. That was how transparent she was because she wanted me to know everything. It felt as though I was on autopilot moving without thought as my body just took over. Was I going crazy because this feeling was all so new, yet so overwhelming that it sprung me into actions that I had never thought about previously? I could not ever in twenty-nine years remember having thought of being remotely interested in pursuing my biological parents. It was almost like having an out-of-body experience watching myself going through these motions still wondering and yet knowing at the same time, what is she doing? Again, the flashbacks of all the times my mother flat-footed and eyeball to eyeball asked me if I was ready.

Reflecting on each time the answer was no. Now wondering if she thought I was saying no to spare her feelings or if I had some underlying reason that I was hiding from her. The truth is it was just never an interest. It was never something that I gave a lot of thought, I was happy. My family was family and that was just that. I desired to know about my health history. Quickly approached the Dirty Thirty and was just viewing things differently. Not sure if this holds for every adoptee but as you get older and for me approaching thirty; things looked different.

Thirty for me was like a light bulb shining so bright it made you pay attention to your life and where you were in life as it measured against the goals previously set. Clarity came in the form of what I wanted to do professionally. My needs from a relationship perspective became clear and dominant for the first time in years. In areas of my life where I was doing things to appease others; I somehow found the strength or know-how to just stop without explanation. At thirty my happiness triumphed over everything. Heavily involved in community service projects and health initiatives was now in my face because of the work I did through my Sorority, none other than The Illustrious Delta Sigma Theta Sorority, Incorporated. Thoughts began to develop around what sicknesses could I be predisposed to. Did I have a higher probability of possibly being susceptible to such conditions as high blood pressure, diabetes, or cancer of any form just to name a few? When you are adopted, this can end up being a major influence on the wanting to know your birth parents and family, if for no more than having that knowledge of family genetics. I wish that there were some ways for agencies responsible for overseeing the adoption process to obtain this data early in the process. This piece more than anything drove the entire process for me. It is not the same for everyone. I can imagine that some just want to know their biological family period. No reason other than just wanting to know. This is a natural feeling and response when you know that there is a whole set of people on this earth that you are related to, and you have no idea who they are and where they are geographically. Perhaps life is good, but you somehow feel it would be better just knowing who they are and having that connection. Being able to feel whole is a proper descriptor. You look at your friends, colleagues, and other family members thinking they all know their birth parents, siblings, cousins, nieces, and nephews. In life with anything be careful about comparisons. When you compare your life to others always remember it is not always as it seems. This is very unhealthy behavior. In your eyes, you may believe that people are aware of who their birth family is, but it could be that the aunt is the birth mom. The dad may be the neighbor down the street or around the corner. If we are honest families have secrets that they will take to their graves. There are so many that have adopted children or did not go through the legal process to do so but raised the child as their own and have never shared with the child the circumstances of their very being. It is my humble opinion, that this behavior is the beginning of placing a negative stigma on adoption and the way that drove the decision. What is the point of hiding it? Who and what is it serving? In most cases, it was an intentional process if not just outright necessary. Protecting and wanting the best for a child is never wrong. Doing the right thing is always the answer no matter how difficult or uncomfortable it may be for you.

A child is helpless and has no choice in choosing their birth parents. To this day I and many can confirm that the minute the words leave your lips "I am staying for the children" I always say why? You are unhappy and it shows. There is no reconciliation or reviving of the relationship, and it shows. I believe in Heaven on earth, and I fight to live like it at all costs. The children did not choose the parents so do not blame them for remaining in a broken relationship that is not repairable. When you do this, you are teaching them that your misery and misery in and of itself in relationships is normal. When in fact it is not. Happiness and internal peace are real. So never blame the children, finances, and appearances of happiness on the children because those are not and were not their choices. In the same vein, I say it is possible to work through problems, and disagreements and reconciliation are possible and real. So do not hide adoption from the adoptee. Ultimately it crushes their foundation and when that is broken finding stability becomes even more out of reach. Not impossible but more difficult.

CHAPTER SIX

THE NEIGHBORS, FAMILY, AND FRIENDS

Might not have mentioned it earlier but I remember the level of nosey I grew up with and I do not care if you leave for two years or twenty-two years and show up with a baby somebody somewhere is going to know the origin of that birth and how you came to miraculously show up with a child. And they are always waiting in the wings to share your secret. However, you view it in your mind hiding it is never a good choice. Therefore, I strongly encourage parents to be honest as early as possible if they adopt a child or raise a child that they did not give natural birth. Tell them. They deserve to know how they came to have the life you graciously gave them. More importantly, you want it to come from you the one who loves them unconditionally and sacrificed to ensure they were loved and provided for daily. Not that person whose intent is not pure or that person who will deliver it with malicious intent. Do not make it good or bad just that it is and it's nothing wrong or negative about it.

You are scheduled to speak!

I met my biological sister, Danielle approximately a month after my initial inquiry. We both learned together that our biological mother was agreeable to speaking with us by phone. By this time, my sister Danielle and I were visiting regularly. She always came to my place, and it was at my place that we received the notification that we were going to speak with the woman who gave us life and immediately gave us up for adoption. A few days before the arranged conversation via phone, my sister and I learned that this meeting was going to be very delicate. Turns out that although our biological mother agreed to speak to us, she was at the time married and had been for twelve years with a family of her own and they were not aware that Danielle and I existed. For me, that was not a surprise, but I could see Danielle did not take it well. It was something about the expression on her face when the Social Worker made the statement. You could tell at that moment that somehow it was another rejection or possible letdown in her mind that would manifest itself much later. I saw it and did not quite recognize what I was witnessing at the time primarily because I was trying to digest my thoughts and reconcile my feelings. Not a total surprise to me that her family was not aware. Yet trying to understand why she reached out all those years ago. What was her end goal? One can only assume that when she did not hear back, and nothing became of her inquiry she decided to continue living with the secret. Based on Danielle's reaction it was then that I realized we were on this path for vastly different reasons. I was never clear on what drove her desire to want to pursue this but for me, my driver was crystal clear.

CHAPTER SEVEN

THAT FIRST PHONE CALL WITH HER....

The call is all scheduled. Danielle and I are at my place a small one-bedroom, one-bathroom apartment that I loved. To date, it is one of the sexiest floor plans ever. We were standing at the bar off the kitchen waiting for the phone to ring and it did. On the other end was this voice that nervously said, hello this is Avery. Danielle and I both smiling reciprocated. We were like two little kids in a candy store and were told we could have anything we wanted before leaving. The fact that it was happening. All from a single phone call. We are now speaking to the women who gave us life. Our voices were the same, speaking mannerisms were noticeably similar. Small talk and pleasantries were exchanged, introductions were made so she would know from her end who was speaking and by the end of the call, we were somewhat shell-shocked. After hanging up we stood there in silence looking at each other. Both certainly thought about what had just happened. The words Avery spoke that resonated with me was that she always prayed that she would meet us before she turned fifty. Some people have nervous energy and will laugh or react in a way that is outside of character or inappropriate in some circumstances. This was a very intense moment and I have no history or knowledge of who Avery is as a person. Of all the things you could say that statement just did not register on my list of options. It did not give me a level of comfort; it gave me pause. I instantly felt the wall go up and I think it stayed up for a long time. The call may have lasted for five to ten minutes or so before it ended. Now, what is next? Although Avery was agreeable to speaking with us, she still had not shared our existence with her family. It has now been a month since we started this process. Danielle and I have been in the know about this potential reunion. How do you almost thirty years later while sitting at the dinner table randomly say - Hey! I have two daughters that I gave up for adoption almost thirty years ago. I never knew that they would one day surface, but they have. We spoke via the phone earlier this week and it was a great conversation. We ended the call thinking we should all meet soon. Pass the cornbread please and sips tea. That would be overwhelming for anyone.

Approximately three weeks after we all first spoke over the phone; we were called by the agency informing us that we each had to pay a fee for them to arrange for us to meet in person at the facility. Now, this was a surprise to me that I had to pay an agency that facilitated my adoption, arranged for me to meet the first identifiable biological family member at no cost; has now decided to charge me a fee to meet the person whose decision started this entire path of events. Why are you now charging me a fee to arrange a meeting for willing participants? Not to mention we have already had one meeting at the facility and there was no charge. And the analytical me started with the questions again. Why are you charging me? What if someone cannot afford your fee? How could this be handled better? Will they agree to this? Am I about to have to pay for one or possibly both? The turnaround to get the answers were quick, we all agreed and were all able to pay the fee. Now that we have settled that obstacle what is ahead?

CHAPTER EIGHT

THE BIG DAY HAS ARRIVED.

IT IS TIME FOR THE US TO MEET!

It was approximately six in the evening, and we had all
arrived. Nervousness and anxiety took control of me all that
day. How I got anything accomplished at work is still a blur.
Again, it was not a thought process about what to wear that
day, hair done, nails done, make-up moderately applied.
Back then the hair and nail appointments were standing.
Same time, same place, the same day of the week. I threw on
a suit just like before because back then that was all I ever
wore. It was officially Fall my absolute favorite time of the
year. Darkness settled in earlier than usual. Our meeting was
so late in the day due to everyone needing to complete their
workday. Now I am a veteran at this. Know where I am
going and have met at least one of the parties involved. The
layout of the building and hallways are familiar. But OMG!
What if I bump into her on my way inside? Lord GOD,
please do not let that happen. What would I do? What do I
say? My mind is racing, and my nerves are completely shot.
My parents met me there again on this day as they did the
first time for my first meeting with Danielle. No doubt they

were just as anxious and nervous as I was that day. We were all escorted to individual holding rooms and waited for everyone to arrive. I may have been in that waiting room for all of ten minutes, but it felt like an eternity, and then it happened. The Social Worker, Kelley came in and said everyone is here and we are ready. At that moment, feeling faint may have been the perfect descriptor, but my legs allowed me to stand and put one foot in front of the other to walk into the next room where everyone else was already assembled. Let us go next door and make introductions. Unbeknownst to me my parents and Avery had already met in the parking lot. Turns out my dad realized he had a flat tire upon arrival and decided to fix it before the meeting and Avery parked right next to them. You would have to know my dad to know he knows no strangers. His first words to Avery were nobody needed to tell me who you are because I already know. My baby girl looks just like you. They had been visiting and talking for a few minutes before entering the building and my entry into the room where everyone was already assembled. So, as usual, I was the last to arrive at the party. Everyone was gathered and talking as though they had known each other for years. This brought tons of comfort to me and just like that a total feeling of calm settled and it all felt right.

We enter the room, and it was no doubt or guessing games as to who is who? My biological mother Avery and I were spitting images of each other. What was even more breathtaking was how much the daughter that accompanied her and me looked alike. Her name was Kasey, and before this day she proudly wore the title of big sister and our arrival at least for that day stripped that away. I could not stop staring at her the resemblance was so uncanny. She was just a much younger much thinner version of me. The entire experience was so surreal, to say the least, but there was a level of relief as well. It was a true exhale moment. Relief that I did not even realize I wanted or needed to present itself with a huge bang. We exchanged pleasantries made introductions and hugged; it was an instant family reunion. At least on the surface.

Over the next few months, Avery and I would talk on the phone and meet out often for dinner. Things were going so well as time passed Avery was invited to hang out with me and my girlfriends multiple times. Avery too looked quite young, and it was never new for one of us to bring a girlfriend that was unfamiliar to the group for a girl's night out. It may have been a few days later when a discussion of the previous last girls' night out was brought up. It was at this point that I divulged who Avery was and if you could have seen the look on my girlfriend Dominique's face when I told her that Avery was my birth mom and that we had just met a few months earlier. It was priceless because she thought she was just another girlfriend of mine hanging out. Then she took the time to look at the pictures and reflect on the night and was like OMG!! You do look just like her. Dominique and I met at Prairie View A&M University while modeling and have been tied at the hip ever since. She has been there from the beginning. She has seen the best and the worst of my life experiences. The meeting and integration of Avery, the birth of my daughter Neely Simone, was a Bridesmaid in my wedding, all the way through my mother's transition in 2018 and so much more in between and to date.

Now that we have all met my parents were eager and incredibly open to integrating Avery and the rest of her family into ours and I was equally as eager to do the same. On several occasions, my parents extended multiple invitations to Avery for dinner at their home. Each time she accepted, and we would enjoy dinner and get to know each other in my parents' home initially. Things were going well. Everyone seemed to be settled in and things were comfortable and genuine. A few more weeks passed after we had several dinner engagements and then the big reveal was arranged. Avery finally found the courage to share with her family that both Danielle and I had miraculously turned up and she wanted everyone to meet us. It was equally impressive that the younger sister Kasey was able to contain this secret having met us already a few months prior. And as easily as every other detail had been arranged and seamlessly executed so was the family meeting.

We met at one of Avery's older sisters' homes who to my surprise was a Human Resources Director at a local-global Oil and Gas Company in Houston. Referring to her affectionally as Aunt Tutu, she was more than happy to host the forty-five family members that we were able to attend. Talking about bizarre and just an overall surreal experience is to walk into a room of forty-plus people that you do not know and have never met, but you look like a vast majority of them. The feelings were overwhelming and the entire time constantly reconciling in my mind that this is happening. Reflecting on that day there was no way possible to orchestrate the events as they unfolded. Introductions were done hugs and smiles were exchanged pictures were taken, food and drinks were plentiful and then the "do you know?"

conversations were had. On this day I went from being the youngest of two to being the oldest of six. My biological mom gave birth to five girls, me, Danielle, Kasey, Keisha, and Kenya, and one son, Kendrick. The parallels between the family that raised me, and Avery's family were jaw-dropping. My dad had eight sisters and seven brothers. Avery had nine sisters and one brother. Here I am well over one hundred cousins on my dad's side of the family and a minimum at that time of forty plus cousins on my mom's side and meeting another forty plus relatives from my birth mom's family. There are just no words and the biological father discussions had not even surfaced just yet.

Avery's oldest sister lived a few blocks over from some close friends of my parents, whom we visited often throughout the years. After many conversations, it was discovered that Avery was a Florist by trade and worked for a popular grocery retail chain not far from where I interned during the summers for college break. Turns out Avery was the florist for the Judge that I interned for over the summers and all the beautiful floral arrangements that I would see throughout the office every summer were all done by my biological mother. All these years we were within a stone's throw of each other. And to take it up a notch we lived within a fifteen-mile radius of each other as well. The world is a huge place but that year it got extremely small. Time passed and we continued to talk and meet up from time to time. After my experience with meeting Avery and the rest of the family and going through this process, I felt it was my duty to give back in some way.

My parents and I sat on a panel at Depelchin Children's Center to talk about our experience to give hope to those that wanted to adopt and some level of peace to those that had given up children for adoption. Sitting on that panel you could see the mothers who were broken. Their spirits were broken because they had given up a piece of themselves. Not knowing or having any clue about where the child is and if they are okay. I witnessed mountains of regret and saw hurt equivalent to that of losing a loved one to death on one side. And then on the other side seeing parents who were so desperate to have a baby. Clinging on to the very possibility that their opportunity to be parents would come from this process. Knowing it is their only hope as all other avenues had been exhausted. And then here we sit, intact, happy, and eager to share our feel-good story of success. Offering hope and some level of comfort to total strangers.

This experience for me was a good one and very eye-opening to the many views others have about adoption. Everyone involved in the process is impacted in some way. In my case, it was a perfectly great union. It is my understanding from some that this is not always the case. Rejection is a reality. It is a hard truth for anyone that goes down the path of seeking your birth parents. Once people move on and have conditioned themselves to either forget or pretend that the entire birth and giving up of parental rights did not happen it is hard to unlock those memories. The pain the thoughts and years of buried feelings rushing back is not an easy thing. I caution anyone pursuing or thinking about pursuing this path to be open and caution that the results may not be what you fantasized or envisioned them to be. This is not to discourage anyone from seeking out your birth family at all. It is a natural desire and should not be taken lightly. But you should know that you could be welcoming someone or many people into your life that are possibly not desirable or that are not aligned with your values and ethical compass.

95

CHAPTER NINE

RELATIONSHIP GOALS, WHERE DO WE GO FROM HERE?

For a little under a year or so things seemed to be moving along and settling wonderfully and comfortably for all. Spent quite a bit of time continuing to get to know Avery and Danielle as they got to know me as well. Again, we went out a lot, but I noticed that it was always just Avery. Danielle was married and did not get out much at the time but kept in close contact via the phone. It was never my siblings, never any other newly introduced family members. Avery and I probably went out at least once every week for months, sometimes more, mostly on the weekends and it was always just us. It was odd to me and occasionally, it would cross my mind, but I never asked why? Why is it just us all the time? Am I somehow still part of a secret? How could it be that none of the other family members are interested in developing a relationship? But for months a full year or so after our initial meeting, we would continue to meet for lunch and dinner, exchange birthday and holiday well wishes, and as much as it seemed normal and okay it was not. There was something very off with this situation for me and I do not know if I should have addressed it immediately. I wanted to address it then, but ultimately avoidance took over and I convinced myself that it was okay. It was normal to inquire as to how everyone was doing whenever we were together. Never once did I ever ask why they never joined us for the countless lunches, dinners, and happy hours.

Turns out after conversations with younger sister Kasey many months later it was revealed that Avery was not sharing how often we were meeting and interacting at all with the rest of the family. They had no clue about our interactions specific to the countless lunch and dinner dates. This was all new for her and would be news to the rest of the family. All they knew was we met for the first time and that was the end. There were never any discussions of continuing a relationship beyond that meeting. So, although we had the family meeting where I met uncles, aunts, cousins, siblings, and grandparents, there would never be another time that we, them included would all assemble until Avery's mother passed. And even then, it was more of a cameo appearance for me. I felt no connection. By this time, it was crystal clear that my biological maternal grandmother never wanted me. I was an inconvenience to her reputation along with that of her daughter's reputation and financially it was not feasible to provide for another child. This aside I still felt strongly that it was the right thing to do to attend her homegoing celebration and it was a beautiful service. Reflecting on that very decision would be the catalyst that started us down this path. We have all at one point found ourselves so concerned about what others thought of us. Our image and the thought of what others would think has at some point maybe more than a few times drove us to make decisions that we were and are not proud of or that were not in our best interest. According to what I was told it was my maternal grandmother that drove the decision to put me up for adoption. There is no way for these next words to sound anything but rude, nasty, and possibly retaliatory all of which are furthest from the truth of how I feel or have ever felt. But it was the absolute best decision that turned into the greatest blessing and gift from GOD for me and my family. Based on what I know today my life would have taken a different trajectory. No slight to anyone but there is no doubt it would have been quite different. Reflecting on how my siblings seemed to be so dependent on Avery for their very survival. Witnessing the never-ending pattern of moving out and moving in and moving out again and moving right back in again. No one pursued education beyond high school, and I am only talking about the immediate birth family. In the same vein as I reflect on the family I know and grew up knowing as my own it was the same scenario for us. When comparing the maternal and paternal sides you would need a full block to hang all the degrees that ranked up to PH.D. In contrast to the other side where you only had two of forty-plus grandchildren receive a bachelor's degree and one of those two went on to receive a Master's degree. Once you graduated from high school that seemed to be it, you had arrived. Now, this statement may seem judgmental, and some may view it as demeaning, but it is not intended as such at all. This is the place where I would like to emphasize that culture, environment, and values come into play. Differences in how you are raised and what you believe in come into play in a very big way. Those who know me have heard me say many times that it is your life experiences that mold you. That does not mean that if your circumstances are dire you cannot rise above them, but the environment is everything. On the flip side of the coin, we have all seen many reach the pinnacle of their careers and life experiences and then hit rock bottom. No one is immune to ups and downs; it was intended that way to promote growth. You should always take failure and turn it into a learning opportunity, which ultimately becomes a success. Always fail quickly. Don't linger in that space, learn from it, and move on.

Here I am relatively young and only have one point of view from Betty and Michael. I can hear my mom's words now "When you graduate high school, you are going to college". No questions asked, no opinions sought, it is what it is and that is that. So, to discover that no one had an interest or was not pushed to go further was different for me. Independence was all I was ever taught and all I knew. You must be able to take care of yourself one hundred percent. If I heard it once I heard it a thousand times. Anything short of that was different for me. Everyone in my immediate circle who had graduated from college had their own homes or apartments and I cannot think of anyone who still lived with their parents. They worked in corporate jobs; some were married, some were single, and some were even raising young children. Again, this is all I know at the time so guess what? It is my measuring cup for me more than for others around me. Success does not require a college degree and today's millionaires are not even teenagers yet. It is not my opinion that college makes you successful and I know this is a very touchy subject for many. To be clear I know many who have advanced degrees and are not doing well, so there, be clear it is not my opinion that a piece of the paper defines success. But that was what I was taught just like others are taught to go do better than their parents. My parents did not teach me to believe that corporate America was not an option. My daughter Neely Simone tells me today that she would never have a desk job because she does not want to be tied to a laptop and phone all day every day. I must catch myself often and not be her dream killer. I seek to understand her desires of the heart and what she wants to pursue as a career. You must be in sync with yourself and what works for you, it is never a one-size-fits-all. But respect everyone and meet them where they are. If we can do that, we will be so much better as a society.

Fast forward to Christmas around the third year after Avery and I met I recalled going to her home for the first time. There were many nights and evenings after dinner that I dropped her off at home, but this time I was going inside to sit with and visit with her family. December was also her birthday month. It was one of the first times I had ever been in her home. I thought it would be appropriate to at least pick up a Christmas card and to this day I am not big on gifts as much as I am on spending time with family and being in the moment of developing priceless memories. The memories are far more important than any gift that most of us remember at that moment, but more than likely have no idea where the gift is, and the value of gifts and the excitement around receiving them are short-lived and long gone as time passes.

It is a practice of mine to follow my heart and my thoughts were not in a place to buy a gift or give her money. But I did feel it necessary and appropriate to acknowledge her with a nice card. Remember we always met out at public venues and never visited our homes aside from my parent's house. Avery always came to my place if we were not meeting at a restaurant, which was where we met most of the time. I arrive and it is super uncomfortable and awkward for me before I even got out of the car. I cannot ever remember having that feeling before, but all my internal alarms are going off that this is not going to go well. I remember praying to the front door asking GOD to give me strength to get through the evening. I don't even think I was breathing when I knocked on the door. There was a level of unexplained dread and fear but somehow, I was able to put one foot in front of the other and move forward. Everyone was super nice and seemed to be excited to see me. They watched my every move and listened intently to my every word, which was not too much. But I could tell this was new and quite entertaining to watch for all that were present. I remember Avery's husband saying, "Wow, you guys look just alike." After we were all seated, I gave Avery her card and told her Happy Birthday and she immediately opened it. Once she opened the card to what I thought was to read it she shook it as though she expected something to fall out. I was immediately taken aback and had never seen this behavior from her before. Not only did it take me by surprise, but it was also so unexpected and rude, quite frankly it hurt my feelings and made me angry all at the same time. I never took my eyes off of her, but it was at that moment that I received a glimpse of the real Avery. She had officially surfaced. I had no doubt all eyes were on me. It was one of those moments where you realize when people show you who they are, yet it is a memory that you want to erase immediately. All this time, I have been interacting with her I never once saw this person or this behavior. It was one of the many times that I experienced hurt, disappointment, and outright shock. And frankly, I preferred the sweet docile woman she wanted me to believe she was but here we are in her home and now she cannot hide who she truly is as a person. No matter how hard people try to hide the true person always surfaces to the top. My insides are screaming how ungrateful and embarrassing still in disbelief that she could be so obnoxiously rude. Before I could finish my thought, she jumps up and runs into the backroom and reappears with a box that she presented to me. Wanting to get past that entire moment not just for me but for her too I accepted the box. I noticed it was not wrapped, no big deal. Me being unassuming no agenda just being cordial accepted the box and opened it. Inside was a beautiful pair of Victoria's Secret pajamas. I was really surprised that she had gone through the effort of buying a gift. Again, to me, it seemed so over the top and premature as we were still finding our way in the relationship. At least I was still trying to figure it all out. Oddly enough, fast forward I would learn a few years later while talking to Kasey that those pajamas were the Christmas gift that she had given to Avery earlier that very same day. I laughed so hard because it was so funny to me and painted a clearer picture for me of some of the many family dynamics.

I visited for a few more minutes as I did not want to overstay my welcome. My sisters and I exchanged phone numbers for the first time during that visit. Three whole years later, I thought it odd, but I own that I never made it easy, and I never pushed to make it happen. And it was not odd that we were exchanging phone numbers, but odd that after all this time we had not done so prior. Afterward, it became immediately noticeable that the calls started coming in regularly. We would touch base at least once or twice a week. Avery became extremely interested in our interactions with each other and would inquire often as to whether we talked and went even further to ask about what we discussed. There was always this controlling outright needing to know about every interaction and conversation with Avery.

CHAPTER TEN

INSIDE FAMILY DRAMA

After several conversations with two of my younger sisters Kasey and Keisha, who grew up in the house with Avery, it became clear that there were many underlying issues within their relationship with her, and even more, clear the abrupt appearance of both me and Danielle the two new sisters on deck did not add much positivity to that dynamic. Turns out that they were unaware that we: Avery, and Danielle were all interacting and visiting regularly. But the calls continued, the small talk was consistent and the do you know and where did you go to school conversations were normal. This went on for weeks, maybe months, and then the calls came that began to blow me away. Not long after the home visit two of my newly discovered sisters called me and asked for money. When conversations start with everybody in this house credit is busted and I need help. It would not take a brain surgeon to know what is following that statement. And immediately following was the request for my signature to co-sign for a car. I had to explain that co-signing was equal to buying and my reply was, unfortunately, I would not be able to co-sign for a car. The second time I was asked for money for an abortion. For some reason, I just did not believe that this was the true reason for the ask. It was so unlike her and completely out of the left field and I certainly did not see this coming. Not long after it was confirmed that it was a false alarm, but to this day I do not believe that was the driver behind the ask in the first place. Thought to myself this is so not cool and tried to figure out why there is such a level of comfort with asking for money, not for dinner or a utility bill but high-priced items. Guessing that it would add extra drama and incentive for me to comply I was told the father of the unborn child was not aware of the situation. As I politely declined, I advised that this was not a discussion that should involve me, but instead the responsible parties.

I share this experience because I am a true believer that you must have a very solid foundation as a human being to handle some situations. Had I gone into this situation throwing caution to the wind, I would probably have purchased a car and paid for a procedure. Had it been just five years earlier, I was not in the position where I would have honestly thought through what I was being asked and more than likely would have said yes to both requests. Not because I wanted to give money for an abortion or co-sign for the car, but because I would have been more concerned about what those asking would have thought about me and more so I would not have wanted to disappoint or hurt anyone's feelings. Talk about a hard spot to be in across the board this was one. Now you compound this situation with someone who has not had enough life experiences and has not discovered their value. It would be a tough spot.

Here I am trying to understand how these new people who are the actual bloodline that I have intentionally invited into my life; and who have willingly come into my life will fit and intertwine with my current life. Never once thought that I would be approached and asked for money. It just never crossed my mind. I am not even sure if they gave any thought to how one it would come across and two just how bad it was to go down that path to ask for money. I think it was a behavior of circumstances and environment more than that of being malicious but with a bit of I am going to try and see what happens in the mix.

You can go into a situation for one reason and things that you do not anticipate can happen that will make you rethink the entire thing. For me, it just seemed to be so inappropriate and now I am in this inquiry of did I do the right thing. Again, I do not think the behaviors were malicious at all, but just the result of a pattern of behaviors established long before I came on the scene. On the flip side of the coin, it was so weird to me that Avery seemed always to want to give me unsolicited money. I would refuse and explain to her that it was not necessary, and she would always force the issue. It was extremely uncomfortable for me because I always felt it was tied to her internal guilt. So here I am with my siblings asking me for money and expressing how everyone around them is broke with bad credit but on the other hand, I have Avery periodically throwing money at me. The contradiction just did not add up. If I did not take the money from her, she would throw it through the window of my car as a drove off as this is what always happened during those occurrences. Although, rare and usually always as we were departing from an outing.

This behavior led me to express how I felt to Avery and during one of our many dinner nights I was very direct in expressing to her that she owed me nothing. In fact, before our initial meeting, the agency asked both Danielle and me to write Avery a letter. The letter was to share with her why we wanted to meet her and to give her a bit of background about ourselves. Danielle and I never shared what we wrote in those letters and still have not to this day. But during that

conversation and reflective of my first and only letter to her
I was truly clear in expressing that I was never upset or angry
about her giving me up for adoption. I felt like it was a gift.
As I reflect on my current life and my maturity, I think that
still rings true today. Saying that my adoption was a gift is
in no way slight or disrespectful. For a young teenager faced
with a decision such as giving up your firstborn is no small
feat. What I wanted to know from her was about her health
history and if there were any underlying health conditions
that I should be concerned about. Unfortunately to this day,
I have not received a straight answer to that question.
Everything with Avery was and has always been very vague
and a mystery and I do believe this is a generational thing.
Our parents and grandparents were truly in the business of
hiding information from children. If I wrote all the things
that I have discovered after the death of family members that
would be a seven-part movie series. Thinking back, it may
have been very presumptuous on my part to think that after
all this time she would share that information with me
knowing how important it was in my quest to find her. But
the reality is she may not have known or just did not want to
say. We will never know and I had to accept that reality.

During this point in my life, a lot is going on. Career moves are happening, I am trying to find my place in Corporate America and gain as much knowledge as I could to get ahead. Constantly ran into situations while working where it was apparent that I was expected to do the work yet needed to be comfortable without being acknowledged for my hard work verbally or financially. In addition, to serving on no less than five committees in multiple organizations leaving my house at 5 a.m. and returning at 11 p.m. was the norm. And to top it all off my relationship was headed to the graveyard where it rightfully belonged. It did not help that I was beginning to wonder if I made the right decision by pursuing this process in the first place and the doubt weighed heavily. For every five steps I made to get ahead in the blink of an eye I was knocked twenty steps backward. My decisions were off and not yielding the intended results. Now sitting in the space of rethinking did I do the right thing? Perhaps leaving well enough alone may have been the route to take. When you are eyebrow-deep in a situation and it is not going as anticipated it is easy to start backtracking.

The flip side of the coin is that my misery in corporate America at the time yielded to me a lifestyle that I loved. Loved the money and the freedom to move around as I desired. Jump on a plane and vacationed whenever I wanted and wherever I wanted in or out of the country. Young and successful, living the dream, Neiman Marcus was my favorite retail therapy spot at the time. Spent quite a bit of time in Neiman Marcus during this season. There was always an event to go to whether it be brunch, lunch, and a gala, or just hanging out with the girls. Living in the cutest bachelorette pad ever! I still get excited thinking about that one-bedroom double-sided fireplace with the jacuzzi tub. Whoever designed that place was incredibly talented. Super sexy would be an accurate descriptor. The sliding mirror wall divider that opened to the oversized bathroom was genius. The mini river walk that lay between buildings and the sound of the waterfalls, always made it sound like it was raining. I got the best sleep while living at that place. All the while still trying to figure out how to make my mark on the world and do good things. How did I get here? How do I get there? Questions I ask myself often.

By this time Avery was still calling, but we were not seeing each other as much. Then out of nowhere, I started hearing frequently from my biological brother Kendrick. He and I were and are so much alike straight shooters not capable of playing games. He spilled his heart out about how he always knew about me. He asked if Avery and he called her by her first name all the time and still does to this day had ever shared with me that we had the same father. I told him yes, she had shared that we had the same father. At the time I did not share with him during that conversation but in my mind due to so many other previous conversations and experiences with her I was not convinced that was true. He said he wanted to confirm that we did have the same father and that I should meet this man he called dad someday. Kendrick even went further and asked me to take a blood test. I was not a fan of the blood test request because knowing was not that important to me. It made me revert to the adoption and how people can put so much emphasis on bloodline, but in retrospect and many can attest to this - it is your bloodline that will and can hurt you the most. A natural bond of love does not require sharing the same bloodline. My thought during the conversation with Kendrick did you need a blood test to accept me? Is that going to be the end all that confirms what our relationship should or should not be? You know we have the same birth mom. Why does the paternal identity mean so much? Now the funny thing about him saying that is a few weeks prior my mama and I had talked about the man named my biological father. And I expressed to her that I did not believe it at all.

If you knew my mom you would know Betty Neely was equivalent to the CIA, FBI, and the Secret Service all rolled up into one and was a one-woman shop. She quickly verified that absolutely that is your biological father, and you look just like'em. Went even further to show me photos of my birth father, and his mama, but when she said, here are some of your cousins. I was just done. This woman had been all on social media and dug up birth records and voter registration information to connect the dots. It was amazing what she could do with such ease. Sat me down at the kitchen table talking about here is a picture of a cousin. Take a good look so you do not end up dating him. And here is another one, looks like she is a professional comedian. It was all too much for my mind to take in at the time. I was like mama please stop just stop. She insisted I needed to know, and she did not want me showing up at her house dating my cousin. Then fear settled in for me because that thought never crossed my mind but was a real possibility. These pictures were of people that lived in the community I grew up in as a child. Age was not a factor that would have kept us from knowing each other. This was a time when I am entering my thirties, was being acknowledged in publications, such as The Houston Chronicle and The

African American Times and a few other local publications and within months I would see an article on one of my aunts where a school was being named after her and articles on another aunt who was married to a prominent Judge in the community in those very same publications. The parallels were just too much to wrap my head around. But my mother who raised me wanted me to know and she was very intentional about it.

As Kendrick and I continued to talk he shared with me that my paternal side of the family always knew about me. This was something that I never knew and was incredibly surprised by just hearing it said out loud. He expressed anger and discontent that is heart-shattering because I could hear the pain and feeling of betrayal in his voice. As he shared how everyone on that side of the family always knew about my very existence and continuously questioned Avery about my whereabouts. As she denied it every single time. It was as though she had erased that part of her life. Turns out our father went off to the service and was fully aware of my expected arrival. Only to return to the States with no child. He did not understand, and things just went downhill from there based on what I was told.

Not long after my brother encouraged me to speak with our biological father and I was able to do so via the phone. His first words to me were that he loved me, and he said he looked for me and he always wanted me. These were his first words over the phone, and they rang through so authentic and powerful. Anyone who would have or could have witnessed that moment could not deny the pain, regret, excitement, and pure joy he felt all bundled up when we spoke for the first time. It was his moment, and he did not mince words. Now even I can see where I got it from. He wanted me to know, he wanted me and loved me and did not understand why Avery took me from him. For some years he thought I was dead. He also said he thought I was a boy. It was as though the entire maternal side of the family pretended my existence never happened. I was never there and never existed. The fact of the matter is it was true, most of my maternal family did not know about my existence. Not sure of the details of how it was concealed so well, but it was done successfully, nonetheless. Kendrick shared with me that Avery had him thinking he was crazy and was losing his mind when he would ask about me. As a child, he is listening to his father and paternal grandmother told him about me, yet his mother continues to deny my existence every time.

There was a whole lot of resentment he felt and experienced because of this.

As a child, it is important to be able to trust your mother. Your mother is the one person that no matter what else the universe has going on if you have her you know that you are and will be okay. And to hear from the paternal side constantly that there was another sibling, yet your mother continues to deny it and say it is not true had to be so confusing for him as a young child. When a mother betrays your trust, you tend to trust no one, or you turn to those that do not have your best interest in mind. Either way, it is life-altering and for some, there is no recovery.

My biological father, Douglass shared with me that he went to Avery's sisters' homes and knocked on doors looking for me. He said that he had been beaten by the husband of one of the sisters for doing so because they did not want him on their property and thought he was drunk, high on drugs, and out of his mind. Now, can you imagine that you are fully aware that you are due to have a baby? Leave for deployment and come back and everyone around you is acting like it never existed. That had to be gut-wrenching. No doubt it was a turning point that changed the direction of his life. It gave me pause to see how decisions can impact the entire trajectory of your life. But Douglass was very apologetic and said that he would love to meet me if possible. Immediately were his exact words. Now here I am, reeling from my experiences on the other side, wondering do I want to add to that. Can I handle more? But I was agreeable to meet. It just so happened that my parents were on travel, and I wanted to talk to them before I popped up and went to meet my paternal side of the family. They had been present for the full experience and I did not want to continue the journey without them. Unfortunately, for me and my hesitation, I was not able to meet my biological father. He died not long after that conversation. Crushed into tiny little pieces was my heart. How could this moment be snatched from me forever after all this time? Why did I let fear and anxiety take over? Douglass had an extraordinarily strong voice; he was extremely high energy, and you could just feel that energy talking to him. I was not aware at the time of his failing health. By the time I called to arrange our meeting he was no longer responsive. I remember the day as though it was yesterday.

His wife at the time answered the phone and I politely and respectfully told her who I was and asked to speak to him.

There was such irritation in her voice when she replied, that he is sick and cannot talk. I immediately felt the need to apologize for disturbing her peace. I felt so bad that I had upset her which was not my intent at all. And then a few days later I realized he never responded to my call. The next call I received was that he had passed away. As I sat in silence there was a moment of what could have been. A flash of the gravity of what was missed all due to hesitation and fear. Fear of the unknown and unfair comparisons. And just like that, the opportunity was forever gone.

My family and I attended his funeral and were able to pay our last respects. Just did not have the strength or desire to view his body at his Homegoing Service. It was something I cannot explain, but to see him lying in a casket was not at all what I wanted my memory of him to be. That in no way depicted the liveliness and boldness of his voice and personality that I experienced during our phone call. So, I held onto that moment and how I envisioned him in my mind on that day. I sat in this church, what we learned to be his family church and as I looked around, I saw the Pastor that baptized me as a child, and he stood and spoke at the funeral. Later it would be discovered that he was a cousin of the family. I saw so many other friends of the family and people from the neighborhood I grew up in and all I could think is how, how could this be? How were we so far apart yet so close and connected in so many ways? What would his thoughts be knowing that his very cousin baptized me at the church where he was the Senior Pastor at the time?

Douglass' mother was so sweet and when she realized who I was it was as though he was speaking to me all over again. She said it was not us we wanted you. And went on to express her excitement that she was able to meet me. Her voice was so soft and reassuring that you could just tell that she was full of love and portrayed that grandparent magic that I grew up with and knew so well. Her reaction to meeting me and the reaction of my biological maternal grandmother when we met, was a stark contrast. It is funny how things pop into your head, and I thought back to meeting my maternal biological grandmother for the first time as I sat in support of my brother and just looked around the room. Thought to myself here I sit with an entire family that I was born into and yet there are only three people in the room I knew personally before my arrival.

But getting back to my first experience with my maternal grandmother. Instead of her just saying hello! Her very first words to me were "it was the right decision". It was very firm as though she needed to reassure herself that it was the right decision. What neither of us was ready for was my reply. And eyeball to eyeball before I even realized it my response to her was yes ma'am it was the absolute right decision. We are in total agreement. She looked not just stunned but stung by my response and her body language was that of someone who had been shocked as she shifted in her chair from the short exchange. The importance of her knowing I felt the same way was necessary. She needed to know I was not looking for anything. So, whatever she thought I was there for I nipped it in the bud immediately. And that was my first and last time ever speaking to her again. She was so cold and not very welcoming at all. I guess it was one of those things where you die on the sword based on a decision you made that you thought was right at that time. And I can wholeheartedly say it was the absolute best decision. But she never in a million years thought her decision almost 30 years earlier would stare her in the face and easily and convincingly agree.

CHAPTER ELEVEN
ACCORDING TO AVERY THE DECISION WAS MADE

According to Avery, it was her mother who took her to Depelchin Children's Center and forced her to live there and give birth. It was her mother that demanded she gives me up for adoption. To date, I have never heard a different explanation, theory, or story. Not that one was needed, but I think her mother's first words to me pretty much sealed the deal that this was a true account. There was a concern of shame amongst the church family and friends. She could not have a young daughter unmarried and having a baby. It just did not look right. As I sit here today and reflect on it all I say Thank you!! Had I not been adopted; I believe my path in life would have been quite different. My experience with Avery showed me that she has a controlling spirit, and it probably has not served her well. In my opinion, somehow, she measured her success by controlling the children she kept and possibly stripped them to some degree of their full growth and potential. This behavior intentional or not is worlds apart from what I saw and was ultimately taught by my parents. They always wanted me to have more and do better in life.

At Douglass' repass, the whispers began, and the glaring started. It was awkward, but I stayed a while longer before I departed. It was important to me that I gave his wife all the respect that I could, so I stayed out of her way and was still able to support my little brother through his grief of losing his father whom he knew and grew up with as a child. On the other hand, it is now for me to reconcile my regret of waiting and not feverishly moving forward to meet him. It still saddens me to this day that we never met because there is no doubt in my mind that it would have been a more palatable experience. One would wonder, did he tell his wife about me? Although I do not think it was a secret in their marriage, I still felt that for her with his passing, my showing up there was just one more thing. Once again, believing GOD planned that me seeing him for the first time would be during his Heavenly sendoff, there was still this lingering feeling that there was some fear Avery had that loomed over me meeting him as well. There is something still lingering that she just does not or did not want me to know.

What I heard from my biological father was something I never heard from my biological mother. She always said she wanted to meet me and Danielle before turning fifty. Never once did she say, she wanted me or Danielle. Now keep in mind, that it was short of a miracle that we were able to go through the process and meet. The understanding from Depelchin Children's Center is that they teach, prime, and guide young expecting mothers to erase the entire experience from their minds. The young pregnant women during this time frame now over 50 years ago were able to live in the facility and get all the medical attention needed up to and through delivery. And after birth, they were allowed to see and hold the baby. In my case per Avery, she too was able to give me a name at birth. So, I get why we may not have continued a relationship that I would label healthy, not because of the name she gave me at birth. But because she was primed to forget that her experience of being pregnant, living in an all-girls home, and giving birth had never happened. Avery shared with me that after she gave me up, she immediately turned around and got pregnant with my brother Kendrick. Of course, Douglass demanded that she see that pregnancy through which gave him a son. Then she shared that she again immediately turned around and got pregnant with my sister Danielle who was also given up for adoption.

The rumor mill behind the third pregnancy is that Danielle's father was married and if this is true then Avery probably felt no choice but to walk that path again and found herself back inside the walls of Depelchin Children's Center certainly trying to figure out how she got there again. I have no direct knowledge that Danielle's conception and the circumstances surrounding her birth are true but the conversations and debates within the family went on for what seemed like months. One thing we know for sure is that it was not the first time such a thing had happened and certainly would not be the last. Once Avery learned that she was pregnant with Danielle at that point she knew the process at Depelchin and was of age to check herself in and go through the process again. Unfortunately, she and Douglass were not able to maintain their relationship. Not even to co-parent Kendrick who was raised primarily by our paternal grandmother. Some years later Avery got married and two more children were born from that union, Kasey, and Keisha she married again and one child, Kenya was born from that union. In a flash, I went from the youngest of two to suddenly be the oldest of six.

But this is my story. Understand that having gone through the process of meeting my maternal biological family I only have a consistent relationship with my brother Kendrick. Danielle and I speak, but not as frequently. However, our relationship is such that we can call and talk as though we talked every day. Kendrick and his family visit and everyone in my close family circle know that he is my biological brother.

Having the opportunity to hear from both my maternal and paternal biological sides of the family was interesting. It gave me a snapshot of just how far apart in thought process, memory, beliefs, and feelings they were about my very existence. It gave me the joy to know that there was a group of people that knew about me and were helpless to do anything to find me but wanted me. And then sadness that another group of people did everything possible to hide and forget about my very existence.

Chapter Twelve

Kendrick, the Baby Brother

Kendrick, my little brother who stands well over six feet tall and is married to the best wife a man could ever ask for has been my shining star in all this once-in-a-lifetime experience. He is my little brother and I love him to pieces. We are so much alike, straight shooters, who put our feelings out there and on display for the world to see. We are one year apart in age. He made it a little rough for me at first wanting a blood test and all, but I think he has advanced enough in his experience with me to know that it does not matter. He and his family have been the true consistency in my life from that initial introduction to meeting my biological family. And on that day that we all met, we probably spent the least amount of time talking and getting to know each other. We have randomly visited and periodically had dinner together for years. It is always a pleasure to be around him, and we have fun and enjoy each other.

I find myself having to constantly encourage him to forgive Avery. Time and time again, I have explained that she was primed and trained to forget that Danielle and I ever existed.

Back then that was the way of Depelchin and how they did things. He and I are fully aware of Avery's need to control everything and everybody. The reality is that the reason Avery and I do not have a relationship to this day that would be deemed healthy is that she cannot control and manipulate me. And she has tried so many times that it is unreal. My internal compass does not do well with manipulative people. And she is fully aware of my position and my feelings regarding her behavior. Forgiveness is something that I have extended to Avery before even meeting her. I continue to encourage Kendrick to forgive her as well. It is the only way he will be free to live his life fully and without the weight of what could have and should have been. We must move forward and make the best of what we have today. I am hopeful that he has been able to start the healing process of forgiving Avery for withholding my very existence from him.

Kendrick was raised primarily by his paternal grandmother as I mentioned previously so he always knew about my existence from that side of the family. Here we are now twenty-plus years later and he shared with me recently that he and the family were moving outside of Houston. This was a complete shock to me because now it will not be as convenient to see them due to the distance between us to see each other as often. It is taking me a while to get used to them not living here in Houston, Texas anymore. Bittersweet it is that I finally get to have a relationship with him and then he just up and relocates out of the blue. Happiness. We are all chasing it, I guess. I am just hoping he finds his peace. His move was so sporadic, and I asked him what drove him to make that decision. He said that no one was talking and he wanted his wife to have that family connectedness that she would never get from Avery and our sisters. He wanted to provide her with some level of normalcy and family; he felt it necessary to relocate for her to have that experience with her side of the family. I thought that was a particularly good decision for him and his family. And ultimately the right decision. Even I get tired of trying to make family be family amongst those that I grew up with all my life.

Who is Danielle?
She is my little sister and still a Mystery.

I have spent a lot of time talking about Kendrick and Danielle. When Danielle and I met as I shared earlier, we hit it off immediately. We talked on the phone a lot we visited at my place for what I felt was healthy for two people just getting to know each other. We were in the same profession and lived close in proximity to each other geographically. She could have been someone that I had seen in the grocery store once or twice. Her personality was gentle and very inviting, but her exterior style was extremely bold. She was a voluptuous young woman, wore big platinum blonde wigs with lots of make-up, and always had the tatas at full attention. She had a style of her own that was far from my then extremely conservative one. We were complete opposites in that regard. She came across as having a big heart and genuinely excited about our meeting and meeting our birth mother. Based on what she shared with me she loved her family and had a great life and relationship with the family that raised her. Her parents who adopted her divorced when she was younger, but she continued to have a relationship with both parents. She had a brother too and they were close and still are to this day. I was never clear as to whether this brother was a result of the union between her parents that raised her or that of a blended family. But regardless of the circumstances, it was crystal clear that they were close and had a great relationship. We never met out at all as I think about it, and I have never in all these years ever visited her home. There have been several occasions when I have invited her to my home, however, she has never been able to make it over. We continue to talk on the phone and maintain a relationship to date. We do not talk as often now, but when we do it is one of those scenarios where we can pick right up catch up and keep it moving. Early on I think I may have been too conservative for her and therefore our only connection was that we had the same birth mom, but for a long while, we were able to maintain a consistent connection. I asked Danielle lots of questions about why she wanted to seek out our birth mom and I do not feel I ever got a straight answer or one that struck me as memorable. It was as if she was on this path with no real reason drive or end goal. But I always felt her expectations were high of Avery and the overall experience around meeting her. There was something, perhaps a feeling as though she was owed something, but that something never manifested in our many conversations. Danielle was and is still very much a mystery even to this day. As I reflect on the early days when we first met, she would always give a general location about where she lived never and the exact location and address. Every time she extended an invitation to me to come to her home something would happen where I never made it and it was always her that would cancel or have a last-minute conflict. I always wondered if she were one of those people that compared herself to others, but she exuded such confidence and high self-esteem so I never saw anything that would make me feel this was the case. Then I thought maybe she is just private. Some people are all about knowing you and having a bird's eye view into your life but will shield you from theirs. As time passed and we got to meet our biological family I begin to feel shut out and literally on the outside looking in and to a degree, I was okay with it for the most part. It was mind-boggling to me that Danielle seemed to have a relationship with the other sisters we recently met, and I did not. It will always remain a mystery to me how that came to be. One of the reasons could be that at the time I was extremely conservative. My persona could have been one of very standoffish and shielded. It could have just been that we did not have a whole lot in common. Perhaps I was too conservative and possibly too guarded for them as I reflect. Did I come across as thinking I was better? It would not be the first time that this has presented itself as a problem or concern for others. Was it a perception that was their reality or was it real? That could be part of the puzzle however, I do not think I will ever know. At one point Danielle and Kasey lived together which to me was like what is happening here? Kasey was one of the younger sisters who were there with Avery when we all first met. By the time I learned of this roommate situation, it was already over, and that part was not a surprise. Then there was a horrible falling out between Danielle and Kasey and suddenly no one was talking, and Danielle and Avery were forever at odds at one point for countless reasons. It seemed like there was some argument or debate between the two of them all the time. All along I am on the outside looking in asking the same question. Are we talking about the same people? My experiences with Avery and my siblings were far from that of Danielle. It seemed that there was always some discord or argument between one, two, or all of them and there was never an end to the madness in sight. As if I was not already going through enough turning thirty and just viewing life quite differently. If anything caused me stress and brought drama into my life, I wanted no parts of it under any circumstances and I did not care if you were family or not. This is probably why; I was immediately an outsider. I am sure my reactions to it shined through and through. For long periods, Danielle and I would go months without talking to each other. We would mostly connect around holidays. When I think about her, or she crossed my mind I made it a point to call and check on her. She also over the years seemed to be very sickly. It was a large range of things from work accidents and car accidents to a medical diagnosis that seemed to be profoundly serious and seemed to be a constant. There was a stint where she was always in the hospital, out for a few days, and back in again. If it was not her then it was a close family member. There seemed to always be something going on with sickness that was extremely excessive for someone so young. After a while, I with zero medical training diagnosed her as a Hypochondriac. This was probably not fair, but it was so much I could not help but land in that space that there was something wrong. It was a constant with multiple surgeries, hospital stays, or recently being discharged from the hospital. Chronic is my only description. Then I began to feel it was an attention grabber because I would periodically talk to my other siblings, and no one would make mention of it ever. There may have been one instance where Kendrick and his wife went to visit her in the hospital, but by the time I would find out about it she would have been released and at home. The cycle was never-ending to me and again, I was dealing with my revelations about life.

After what seemed like months and years of arguing and discord within the birth family Danielle seems to have now reconciled and resolved all the past bickering and fighting that used to occur with our middle sisters and our birth mom.

For me, this is great news because it reflects growth and maturity on the side of all. Most importantly it gives hope that we are all on the same path of meeting each other where we are in the process and offering some level of grace and understanding. I do believe that had we all grown up under the same roof we would all be living a life believing that fighting all the time and constant disagreement and discord was normal and maybe it is, I don't know. I just know I don't like it at all. I am happy for Danielle that she was able to find this place of forgiveness and have a relationship with our maternal biological family. Unfortunately for me, it is sad that I do not have a better relationship with my sisters and although all things are possible only time will tell if that will ever change. See I grew up where you had arguments and disagreed, but it was never all the time or a constant occurrence. Once you had your say, you moved on and it was a fresh start and far and in between before the next time. So, if every time I talk to you, and it is an argument every single time then I moved further and further away from it. Families are not perfect, no one is perfect, but I just hate constant bickering and drama. Growing up practically an only child could be the catalyst to my belief. Perhaps if I had siblings and my brother and I were closer in age it's possible that I would have a different view. I believe that Danielle noticed that this behavior was not engaging to me and at some point, everyone else did too. I began to learn less about what was occurring in that world. And for me back then it was a different world. I just could not relate. I wanted to but I just could not.

I describe myself as an outsider to them more so because my style is and was different because I do not engage much in the cycle of constant arguing and bickering; that was a miss in the bucket of qualifications to fit in, I guess. And here we are years later, and Danielle can still tell me what is going on almost daily with the birth family. And again, I think to myself, how is this possible?

CHAPTER THIRTEEN
REVELATIONS ABOUT MEETING THE BIOLOGICAL FAMILY

My experience with meeting my biological family did not yield the intended result. My thoughts and I strongly believe the thoughts of my parents who raised me was that this new addition would be an extension of our family equal to that of a blended family. We (me) envisioned family gatherings and just added them to the mix. Clearly with my paternal father passing so soon after we spoke this would not be the case. However, it is disappointing that Avery was not able to be in that space of family connecting and embracing the new normal. The odds of us meeting and having an opportunity to be a family with healthy interactions were missed earlier on.

Once she revealed the very existence of Danielle and I you would think forming a healthy relationship would be a catwalk. From all indicators, her family was on board and wondering why it was not happening according to the conversations I was having with my middle sisters. I never heard much from the baby sister. She was so young at the time and just not interested in the hoopla of the two new sisters. She was fine with the two she had already. This I understand because developing relationships that you want can sometimes be hard.

As I have backed away from the situation and reflected on the experiences during that time it is sad. Avery could not accept that she was going to be an extension of my family that raised me. As much as my parents embraced and accepted her the feeling was just not mutual. It could be that she would not have taken that road herself, therefore, although she was living it, she could not believe it as the authenticity that it truly was. It was as though she wanted me to forget about the family that I knew and abandon my thirty-plus years of life before our meeting and just pick up as though it was just us, she, and I and that was just not going to happen.

The heart's desire to know your birth parents is and can be immensely powerful. The mental and sometimes physical toll can be overwhelming for some. But I urge all walking this path to take a realistic self-inventory, understand who you are as an individual, as an adult young or old, and be clear on your values. Although you can daydream what the beauty of reuniting can be, the instantaneous love and acceptance. Beware that you can be met with the exact opposite, and I cannot stress that enough. Things shift and change, it's exceedingly difficult and takes effort on both sides to intertwine families that set out on paths that are so different, based on quite different needs. You have a young mother who is faced with giving up a child. Her parents may have mandated that decision, or she may feel that based on her desires and life decisions, it is just not the right time to take on parenting, emotionally or financially. Just keep in mind that regardless of the reason, you may very well want to have a relationship and instant family, but the parent, may not want to acknowledge or face the reality of the decision that was made years prior. The pain and in some cases guilt of that decision can bring back a lot of feelings that were never intended to rise and see the light of day ever again.

As beautiful of what could be deemed a seamless process of reuniting, years later my biological father has passed, as has my mother who will always be mama to me, who raised me. And I have not spoken to Avery in several years as of the penning of this book. When you are trying to incorporate another family into your life, just understand that it is not instantaneous and there is not a magic wand that will make it all pretty and perfect. At the end of the day, we are all people with different views, needs, and wants. If you are allowed to meet your birth family and all sides are willing to come together and grow together, it can be a beautiful thing. I encourage those seeking to grow their families to consider adoption. It can be the most fulfilling and beautiful blessing that you will ever experience.

Adoption is highly encouraged. It seems that most want to adopt babies but consider adopting an older child. They are just as deserving and in need of your love, guidance, and family unit. This work has allowed me to share my story. I hope it has helped someone.

Dear Adopted Child,

Embrace your power and special place in this world. Know that you are a part of a very elite group, the CHOSEN. God saw it fit that your life is filled with love and stability that only the one or two parents that sought to have you could offer. Your adoption was a blessing and could have been the springboard to offering you a head start on a very productive and successful life, free of hardships and obstacles that were out of your control. Never view the mother who gave you up as anything other than the angel that she truly was to make that exceedingly difficult decision. She made that decision out of necessity, but mostly out of love. Be grateful to her, because she had the wisdom and maturity to ensure you had a better life. One that she could not give you. Pray for her, lift her in prayer honor her for being that rock at that moment.

If you ever find yourself in the position to meet her, make sure that internally you are in a space of acceptance, appreciation, forgiveness, and gratitude. If you find that you are hurt, angry and disappointed please reflect on the blessings of your life. Did you have one or two parents that loved you, provided for you, and paved a way for you to succeed? Do not forsake that life thinking it could have been better, if only. If only, you were not adopted? As the old saying goes, the grass is not always greener on the other side, and you never know what you had until things appear and you have what you did not ask for or desire. It could be that you were saved from poverty, exposure to drug and alcohol dependency, and abuse of many kinds. So, do not judge, find a way to forgive and love.

Forgive, appreciate, and admire the strength. Be thankful.

Dear Birth Mother and Birth Father,

Thank you so much for your wisdom. This decision, no matter the circumstances that led up to it was heroic. You were able amid so many things to see that you were not able at that time to give the lifestyle, emotional and financial needs required to raise that child and offer a comfortable life. Your maturity to accept the circumstances and make the decision to give up your baby to a family that would be able to provide is one of the most important and unselfish life decisions you could have ever made.

Hold your head up and high, and forgive yourself if it is guilt and grief that you are still carrying. Forgive those that rallied for you to make this decision, even if it was not yours alone. Just know that you made the right decision. And if ever faced with the opportunity to meet your birth child, who has been raised by another family, please embrace that family, and look at them as an extension. Especially if they extend that courtesy to you and even if this is not the case. Do not make that child feel as if they must choose at this stage in the game. It could be the difference between continuing a relationship or not.

You made the decision. Do not show up expecting to instantly have something that you did not earn or sacrifice to have from the start. Understand that like all things relationships take time to build. Be patient, be open, and be clear that the child is not aware of your journey to this point.

Forgive yourself and offer nothing less than respect and love to the parents that gave their all to raise their child, which was the greatest gift you could offer.

You made the right decision!

Dear Adoptive Parent(s),

Thank you for your gift of adoption. You are the angel(s) sent by GOD to love, provide, and care for that child that is yours. Although not from your belly, your heart. Your love is more powerful than any bloodline. Bloodline does not define love and your journey of being a parent is a blessing. Giving a child a life of love and second chances, springboarding them into success, stability, discipline, and consistency is priceless. My advice to you is to never hide the adoption details from your child. The earlier you tell them, the better. Remember, it is not a good thing or a bad thing, it just is, and they will so appreciate the honesty upfront. You hide it, I can guarantee you someone else, most likely a family member is waiting in the wings to tell them and will not give it a positive spin or explain it as well as you can and should. Do not give anyone that power to hurt the one you vowed to protect and love. Share the details and be honest. Never be afraid of the birth parents showing up and developing a relationship. Although it can be good, and sometimes may feel as though you are now on the back burner, just know you are not replaceable. All the lessons, experiences, sacrifices, and love that you have taught and instilled are there and will manifest when necessary.

Allow those family members to be extensions to the family, so long as they have good intentions and are there for the betterment of all involved.

One Very Blessed Adopted Child,

THE CHOSEN

ACKNOWLEDGEMENTS

Thank you to the Most High, my Lord and Savior Jesus Christ for making all my imperfections perfect in your sight.

Honoring my mother and father, Betty and Michael Neely, for your unwavering love, guidance, and support throughout my life; and extending that love and guidance to those in my circle of friends as though they were your own as well. I am ever so grateful for the seventy-six years GOD allowed my mother to be on this earth. I miss her so much; may she continue to rest in eternal peace. Thankful that I am still able to enjoy, celebrate and learn from my dad who is still here on this side of Heaven.

To those strong Super "A" Personality women whom I love dearly. Dominique Davis Sanders, Kimberly Shoaf, Micquell Wallace, G'Ann Jones Blair, Cynthia Parks Jefferson, Tonia Alexander, Michelle Rodney, and Dora Braggs Byrd: Thank you all for being genuine in your feedback and honesty about this project and for your unwavering commitment to serving as my accountability partners.

A special thank you to Antoinette Sheppard for your constant support and love. You were there from the very beginning and were able to give a snapshot into those early days of my arrival.

To Dorita Hatchett, had you not introduced me as a Published Author on your birthday back in 2019, I would hate to think that I may not have arrived here, as it was then a mere eight years later that I spoke the words of my desire to pen this book and the account of my journey to you. Those very words resonated with me that day and I knew then I had to get to work.

To Onedia Gage, What can I say? I applaud you for taking on managing me and all my emotions during this project and keeping the needle moving. You have pushed me to dig deep and move forward, forcing me to visit spaces I did not realize existed. Thank you for your guidance and patience, I deeply appreciate your commitment to me and the successful launch of this book.

Thank you to my wonderful husband Reginald A. Wilson and my beautiful daughter Neely Simone for your support and patience. Thank you for understanding all those long nights and early mornings I needed to put all my attention towards this first-time experience of authoring a book. This was not easy, but necessary for me to achieve my internal desire of helping others. Kevin Green, thank you for stepping in and just supporting me daily as well.

Thank you to those not named who have encouraged me and to all who will support this movement and embrace my story. There are no words to describe the gratitude that I so deeply feel for you all.

ABOUT THE AUTHOR

After reading this, there is not much more to add, however, understand that she is passionate about love and family, connection, and wholeness. Because of her family dynamic, she believes in trust and authenticity. She is the very definition of love and how to make it out of what appears to be nothing.

To reach Michelle Neely Wilson for speaking or conference appearance information, please email mwilson@michelleneelywilson.com.